Geo. C. T[...]

W. H. Behr

Fowler & Simpson
r. Robert Fowler

Robt Hunter

Charles B. Macdonald

H. S. Colt.

LINES OF CHARM

Brilliant and Irreverent
Quotes, Notes, and Anecdotes
from Golf's Golden Age Architects

EDITED AND COMPILED BY
GEOFF SHACKELFORD

SPORTS
MEDIA
GROUP

SPORTS
MEDIA
GROUP

Copyright © 2005 Geoff Shackelford.

All rights reserved. No part of this book may be reproduced in any manner without the express written consent of the publisher, except in the case of brief excerpts in critical reviews or articles.

All inquiries should be addressed to:
Sports Media Group
An imprint of Ann Arbor Media Group LLC
2500 S. State Street
Ann Arbor, MI 48104

Printed and bound in the United States of America.

09   08   07   06   05   1   2   3   4   5

Library of Congress Cataloging Data on File.

ISBN-13: 978-1-58726-260-9
ISBN-10: 1-58726-260-6

Book and dust jacket design by
Somberg Design / www.sombergdesign.com

PREVIOUSLY BY GEOFF SHACKELFORD

The Riviera Country Club:
A Definitive History

The Captain

Masters of the Links (Editor)

The Good Doctor Returns

The Golden Age of Golf Design

Alister MacKenzie's Cypress Point Club

The Art of Golf Design (with Mike Miller)

Grounds for Golf (with Gil Hanse)

The Future of Golf

CONTENTS

Introduction 7

Golf and Architecture 11

The Old Course at St. Andrews 21

Links 31

How the Game Torments the Adventurous Soul 37

The Architect 45

Standardization and Local Knowledge 57

Planning and Construction 65

Upkeep 77

Strategy 87

Hazards 101

Water Hazards 111

The Golfing Landscape 117

Trees 123

The Redan 131

Approaches and Greens 137

Blindness 147

Slipping into the Rough 151

Committees, Players, and Criticism 157

The Ball Problem 167

Appendix—The Architects 175

Sources 181

Acknowledgments 183

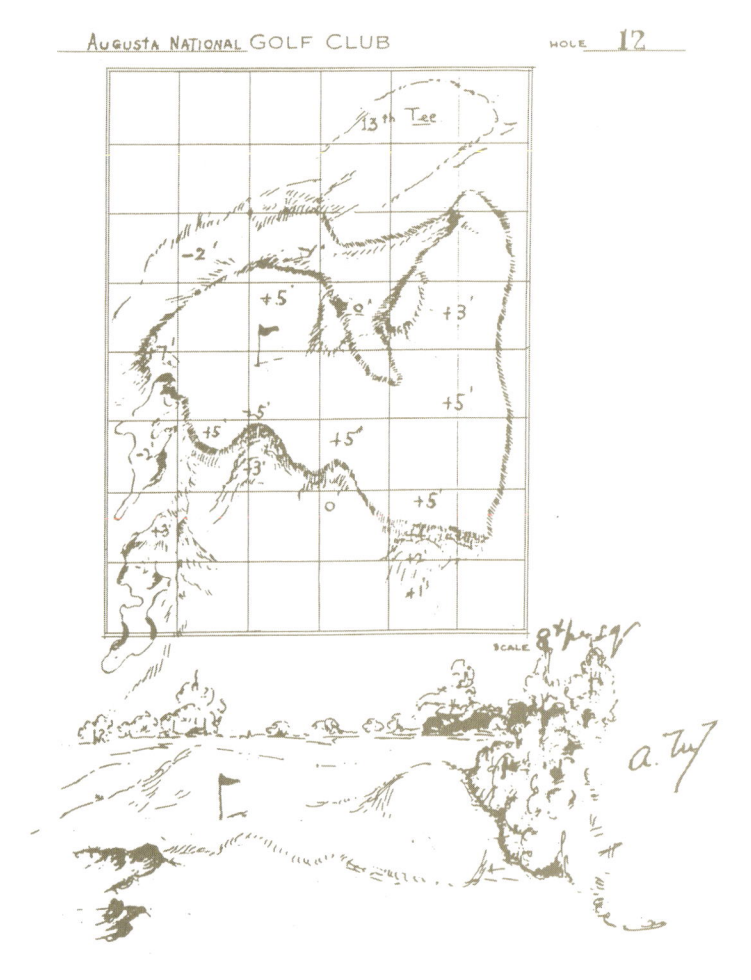

Alister MacKenzie's Plan for the 3rd Green, Augusta National
Originally the 12th hole, this short par-4 green is one of the most unusual MacKenzie created. MacKenzie wrote that "This green is situated on an interesting natural plateau. The left hand side is very narrow; whereas the right side is broad. It is easy for anyone to reach the wide portion of the green with their second shot but difficult to reach the narrow end where the pin will usually be placed."

INTRODUCTION

... no hole is a good one unless it has one or more hazards in a direct line of a hole. Max Behr, who is one of the best American golf architects, states that the direct line to the hole is the line of instinct, and that to make a good hole you must break up that line in order to create the line of charm.

—ALISTER MACKENZIE

No fraternity of characters was more charismatic, literate, or humorous than the architects practicing golf course design from the turn of the twentieth century until the Great Depression, when the Bobby Jones–inspired golf boom came to an end.

Culled from a variety of sources, the following quotes, notes, and anecdotes reveal the brilliance of the game's most eccentric artists: the master architects from golf's "Golden Age."

From late 1910, when C.B. Macdonald's National Golf Links of America opened, to 1937, when the first nine at Prairie Dunes was completed, several timeless masterpieces were built in the United States: Pine Valley, Augusta National, Pebble Beach, Cypress Point, Merion, Pinehurst, Riviera, and Oakmont, to name a just few.

> The novice student of golf course design should find this to be a relatively pain-free entry into the fascinating art of architecture.

Many more classics were recognized as unique architectural venues thanks to rankings or major tournaments: Bethpage, Somerset Hills, Crystal Downs, Prairie Dunes, Southern Hills, Winged Foot, Baltusrol, Seminole, The Country Club, and Shinnecock Hills. And the list of hidden gems spans the entire United States, ranging from Eastward Ho! on the tip of Cape Cod, to southern California's Valley Club of Montecito.

Then there's the group of lost courses we can only imagine playing, the missing or severely rearranged links: Timber Point, Lakeside, Mill Road Farm, The Lido, Sharp Park, Bel-Air, and Fresh Meadow.

All of the aforementioned masterpieces were envisioned by the architects quoted in this book.

By no means does this collection provide a complete representation of each architect who ever offered an opinion during the "Golden Age" of golf design. Instead, this is a compilation of the best things written by architects noted for their courses and their insights. Some names you will know; others may seem anonymous. The only qualification required for inclusion was a design credit to the architect's name and eloquent thoughts worth savoring.

Just as an enduring design proves fun for the beginner while still challenging for the scratch golfer, this book hopes to provide something for everyone.

The novice student of golf course design should find this to be a relatively pain-free entry into the fascinating art of architecture. Biographical sketches are offered in the Appendix so that you know something of the voices behind the classic lines shared here.

For the architecture aficionados who may have read the key volumes and articles used as the basis for this collection, *Lines of Charm* will serve as a useful tool in locating those great lines you remember reading but never can locate.

Readers often struggle to find quotes they are looking for in the classic architecture writings, perhaps because no one wants to dog-ear the pages of these handsome volumes, or most likely because the books provide so many distractions: photos of dynamic holes, drawings that capture your imagination, or prose that went unappreciated in a previous reading.

Provided next to the great "lines" are original drawings of famous holes, construction plans, architect caricatures, cartoons, advertisements, and other period pieces that reinforce our impressions of the dynamic and creative era in which these artists worked.

Ultimately, *Lines of Charm* is here to remind us how fortunate golf was to have so many rich, imaginative, and humorous minds breathing life into the early golf landscape.

Franklin Booth's *The Sahara*
at the National Golf Links

GOLF and ARCHITECTURE

"A friend, who, although not a golfer, was on the whole an impartial and appreciative critic of games, retailed for our edification with great gusto the other day the story of Colonel Pepper calling out to the woman sauntering across the fairway with an infant in her arms—'Now then! Hurry up with that baby of yours,' and receiving like a flash the answer—'Baby yourself, playing with that little ball and in them knickers!'"

As architect Tom Simpson and writer H.N. Wethered recalled, "the only regrettable defect is that Colonel Pepper's answer has been lost to posterity."

The story was recounted in their seminal book *The Architectural Side of Golf*, to suggest "how uphill the battle the votaries of golf have had to fight in order to overcome the ignominy attached to them. Possibly in recent years things have improved in this respect and the storm of persecution and disparagement has blown over a little."

Thanks in part to the efforts of the Golden Age architects, golfers no longer are embarrassed to play the Royal and Ancient game. Yes, great players have propelled the sport onto the international stage and deserve credit for elevating golf's popularity.

But those players were inspired in their play by the grand stages where they were provided a chance to display their brilliance.

Creating a dynamic arena for golf seems so simple. All golfers believe they are capable of producing their own St. Andrews.

Yet even with the Old Course as a model, the architects who came along in the early twentieth century were actually engaged in a search and rescue mission. They hoped to restore order after golf had drifted from the linksland model.

With little subtlety or respect for nature, touring professionals designed most of the new courses built during a late nineteenth-century boom. They dug geometric graves and called them bunkers. They placed these hazards off to the sides or as carry bunkers to emphasize justice for the straight shooter.

Fun for the average golfer was not a priority.

America's Golden Age of golf design commenced with the completion of the National Golf Links, honoring the examples of British Isles design pioneers Old Tom Morris, Willie Park Jr., and Harry S. Colt. Design movements on both sides of the Atlantic shared one intention: to re-create the principles that made golf on the Old Course interesting, pleasurable, and unusual each time around.

The first ingredient to insure fun and variety was simple. Gently lay the design onto the landscape instead of disfiguring it.

This well-intentioned approach seems basic, but golfers have always been self-assured in their ability to envision great golf holes, so the Golden Age architects faced a greater fight than they probably bargained for.

Happily for us, the battle forced them to campaign. They needed to sell their ideas and to do it with humor and grace while writing about the virtues and vices of golf course design. Their words endure today.

Early Tillinghast Rendering of Shawnee

A more primitive approach can be seen in this A.W. Tillinghast drawing. Still, the strategy was sound: play over the "Alpinization" and open up a view of the green while reducing how much the road comes into play.

Regarding "Alpinization" Tillinghast wrote, "Several years earlier Peter Lees, the Mid Surrey greenkeeper, together with ex-Open champion J.H. Taylor, gave to the golf world a new scheme of artificial hazards. Mid-Surrey's course in the old deer park at Richmond, England, is very flat and Taylor and Lees greatly improved conditions by digging hollows and throwing up mounds which were covered with turf. These grass hazards, although artificial, were made to appear quite natural and Alpinization, as it was called, has been created in many sections. However, the building of grass hazards was attempted at Shawnee when the course was first laid out and before America knew of the Mid-Surrey idea."

Playing around a golf course is not merely a question of getting around, like traveling over a race course or walking around the block. It's rather a question of taking nine or eighteen separate and distinct little journeys, each of which presents its own distinct pictures and its own distinct problems as part of the grand tour.

CHARLES BANKS

No game depends so much as golf on its arena for success: on an interesting course an interesting game will be played; on a badly planned green the game will be dull.

JOHN LOW

The first purpose of any course should be to give pleasure.

BOBBY JONES

A golf course may be said to have to satisfy, amongst other things, three definite requirements. It supplies the opportunity for the pleasure of practicing an athletic art; it entails the necessity of providing an adequate test of skill and lastly, it is a disciplinary scheme by which the virtuous cannot be rewarded without a penalty being inflicted on the sinner.

TOM SIMPSON AND H.N. WETHERED

■

It by no means follows that what appears to be attractive at first sight will be so permanently. A good golf course grows on one like a good painting, good music, or any other artistic creation.

ALISTER MACKENZIE

■

When you play a course and remember each hole, it has individuality and change. If your mind cannot recall the exact sequence of the holes, that course lacks the great assets of originality and diversity.

GEORGE C. THOMAS JR.

■

The tilt of the green or its molding, the undulations here and there, the position of the bunkers, the openings for certain shots—these are the methods an architect uses to present the problems. Simply to make holes difficult to play is not at all the point. That would be an easy matter, and unfortunately it is too frequently done by the inexperienced. To make them thrilling to play, to make them force you to play certain shots, and even to reach certain positions in order to have a chance to play such shots—these superlatively fine qualities residing in first-rate holes are the result either of exceptionally desirable terrain or the product of an exceptionally talented architect.

ROBERT HUNTER

Golf architecture is not a science. Creatively it is not amenable to measurable knowledge. The failure to understand this is one reason responsible for the dilemma in the minds of most golfers who try to come to a logical understanding of golf architecture and get nowhere.
MAX BEHR

Golf is a game of balance. The man who knows the value of each of his clubs, and who can work out when it is proper to play one and when to play another, succeeds at the game. The ability of a golfer to know his power and accuracy, and to play for what he can accomplish, is a thing which makes his game as perfect as can be; while a thinker who gauges the true value of his shots, and is able to play the shot well, nearly always defeats an opponent who neglects to consider and properly discount his shortcomings.
GEORGE C. THOMAS JR.

Golf is a game which is comprehensive enough to satisfy the different tastes of those who are by nature imaginative; of those, on the other hand, who are intensely rational; or, in the third instance, of those who regard it as a thing to be dealt with politically, controlled and regulated as a matter of statecraft.
TOM SIMPSON AND H.N. WETHERED

The real test of a course: is it going to live?

H.S. COLT

A golf hole, humanly speaking, is like life, in as much as one cannot judge justly of any person's character the first time one meets him. Sometimes it takes years to discover and appreciate hidden qualities which only time discloses, and he usually discloses them on the links.

C.B. MACDONALD

... golf has to do with a form of miniature and open warfare and is on that account subject to an underlying condition of strategy and tactics. The game is something of a triangular contest conducted between one player and another, with the course itself as a third party to be reckoned with as an antagonist, the last of these being the very interesting combatant with whom the architect is primarily concerned. In this sense it is a form of attack and counter attack, because an increased pressure on the part of the player exerts unconsciously a corresponding resistance on the part of designer.

TOM SIMPSON AND H.N. WETHERED

SECOND PRIZE DESIGN.

Raynor's Runner-Up

When *Country Life Magazine* held its 1914 design contest for a hole that would be built at C.B. Macdonald's Lido Country Club, many future architects entered. Alister MacKenzie's design won, and Seth Raynor, who built the course for Macdonald, finished second with this entry. The hole was built as Lido's 6th, and played as a par-5 instead of a par-4. Raynor went on to have a successful design career on his own, but unlike other masters in this book he never put his philosophy in writing.

"I used to think that my ears would grow to be like asses' ears," Raynor reportedly once said. "For I was always stretching them to take in every word that Mr. Macdonald uttered on the subject of golf."

Really good golf holes are full of surprises, each one a bit better than the last. Like a first-rate dinner, as soon as you have finished one course with beaming satisfaction something even better is placed before you.

ROBERT HUNTER

To arouse this zest each hole should have a character of its own. Its physiognomy should be quite distinct from that of its neighbors, and it should be one not easy to forget. Its personality should awaken your interest and cause you to question how best to approach it. It should present some problem to you in vivid form, and, even though that problem may be solved in two or three ways, it should be quite clear from the beginning that a choice must be made.

ROBERT HUNTER

Every golfer worthy of the name should have some acquaintance with the principles of golf course design, not only for the betterment of the game, but for his own selfish enjoyment. Let him know a good hole from a bad one and the reasons for a bunker here and another there, and he will be a long way towards pulling his score down to respectable limits. When he has taught himself to study a hole from the point of view of the man who laid it out, he will be much more likely to play it correctly.

BOBBY JONES

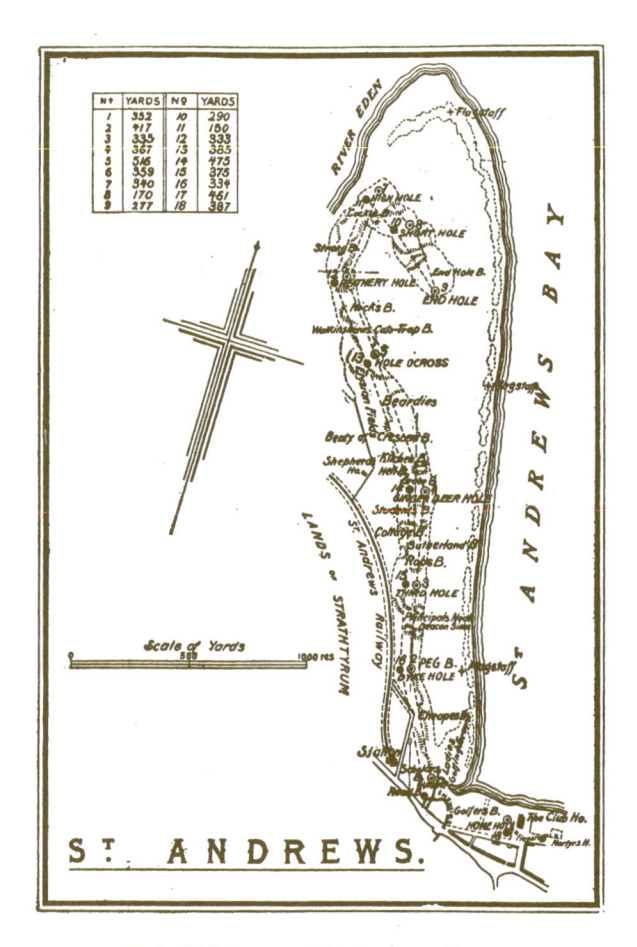

Early Old Course at St. Andrews Survey
Alister MacKenzie believed that "the real reason St. Andrews' Old Course is infinitely superior to anything else in the world is owing to the fact that it was constructed when no one knew anything about the subject at all, and since then it has been considered too sacred to be touched."

THE OLD COURSE at ST. ANDREWS

To have been a fly on the old stone walls of Old Tom Morris's golf shop!

One rainy afternoon in 1898 an eager A.W. Tillinghast loitered around the display of hickories, beloved camera in hand, hoping to capture a shot of Old Tom. He would hang on every word from the game's master greenkeeper, architect, player, and salesman.

Or how about when Dr. MacKenzie stopped in to pick Old Tom's brain about say, the 16th hole? Young Donald Ross was a regular too, picking up hints on greenkeeping and clubmaking.

The young and then less curmudgeonly C.B. Macdonald recalled that Old Tom's shop was the first place he visited when he arrived in town.

"The day I arrived in St. Andrews my grandfather took me to genial and much-loved old Tom Morris and bought me three or four clubs," he wrote in *Scotland's Gift—Golf*. "He also secured me a locker in Tom's shop, for juniors were not permitted in the Royal and Ancient Club."

There is little coincidence in the fact that several future master architects dropped in to visit Old Tom. We can only surmise that these eager students questioned him about the intricacies and maintenance of the Old Course. No person knew the baffling out-and-back layout better than Old Tom Morris, and no one delighted more in sharing his wealth of knowledge than the four-time British Open champion.

Though St. Andrews inspired the great Golden Age architects, would they have appreciated its many intricacies without Old Tom's guidance?

"Old Tom is the most remote point to which we can carry back our genealogical inquiries into the golfing style," wrote Horace Hutchinson. "So that we may virtually accept him as the common golfing ancestor who has stamped the features of his style most distinctly on his descendants."

Hutchinson later dubbed Old Tom "The High Priest of the Hierarchy of Professional Golf."

Macdonald called Morris the "Grand Old Man of golf, the philosopher and friend of all youthful, aspiring golfers."

The Old Course needed a curator like Morris because it was and continues to be peculiar to behold at first sight. The course sits on a mere ninety acres. Today most architects insist on at least 150 acres to build something playable. The Old Course features out-of-bounds down the right side on a majority of its holes and subjects the golfer to several blind shots. Two holes cross each other.

Yet the Old Course still exuded a certain charm that encouraged closer study.

As Robert Hunter asked in an essay titled "The Ideal Course," "Where else in the world do we find a course to which all great players journey and where all ages and abilities meet and praise with equal fervor?"

Nowhere else.

For the architect hoping to create a design worthy of study and discussion, there continues to no better source of inspiration. And once there, the desire to study the course can become all-consuming. Besides, as C.B. Macdonald wrote, "there is nothing to do in St. Andrews but play golf and bathe."

The Old Course at St. Andrews rarely appeals at first sight, and it not infrequently takes years before scoffers succumb to its many virtues … it is a course which caters to a higher standard of golf than any one has attained today, and yet it is extremely pleasurable to the old gentleman who cannot drive a ball any further than a lusty youth could kick one.

ALISTER MACKENZIE

One must take time to know the Old Course in all its moods. One must study the subtleties of its terrain and its curiously shifting winds. One must find its hidden snares and one must approach it without preconceptions of what a golf course should be. To be down the middle may mean nothing there; that may be quite the wrong place. To be long may mean nothing unless length is shrewdly used. To be able to play a few shots perfectly is not always enough; one must at times have the full repertoire.

ROBERT HUNTER

Every opportunity is provided on the Old Course for bringing out the essentials of great golf.

H.N. WETHERED AND TOM SIMPSON

Alister MacKenzie on the 14th at St. Andrews

Alister MacKenzie believed the 14th was unique thanks to the green's marked tilt up from left to right, so much so that it is impossible to approach near the hole from the right.

"Some years ago there were four of us playing four ball matches nearly every day for a month," MacKenzie wrote in *The Spirit of St. Andrews.* "We, according to our judgment, attempted to play this hole in four different ways. 'A' played his tee shot well away to the left of the Beardies onto the low ground below the Elysian Fields, so as to place his second in a favorable position for his approach. 'B,' who was a long driver, attempted to carry the Beardies with his drive, Hell with his second, and run up his third. 'C,' who was a short but fairly accurate hitter, attempted to pinch the Beardies as near as he dare, and then played his second well away to the left, so as to play against the slope of the green for his third. 'D' took what was apparently the straightforward route along the large broad plateau of the Elysian Fields, and eventually landed in Hell or Perdition every time; he invariably lost the hole. This hole is very nearly ideal, but would be better still if the lie of the land were such that the Beardies, the Crescent, the Kitchen, and Hell bunkers were visible and impressive looking. If these bunkers only looked as terrifying and formidable as they really are, what thrills one would get in playing this hole! What pleasurable excitement there would be in seeing one's second shot sailing over Hell!"

St. Andrews still retains its pristine charm. I doubt if even in a hundred years' time a course will be made which has such interesting strategic problems and which creates such enduring and increasing pleasurable excitement and varied shots.

ALISTER MACKENZIE

The pseudo–golf architect will have the faint glimmerings of an idea and will try to catch it with numerous bunkers; whereas the true artist will place just one bunker upon the sore spot and it is done. Such a bunker is the Road bunker in the face of the seventeenth green at St. Andrews. To have placed such a bunker required rare imagination and audacity.

MAX BEHR

St. Andrews has the most perfect golfing hazards which the mind can imagine, but even there these traps are not always successful in catching the bad shots; for the course contains too much good ground outside of the bunkers.

JOHN LOW

St. Andrews yields nothing to power unless it be used with wisdom.

ROBERT HUNTER

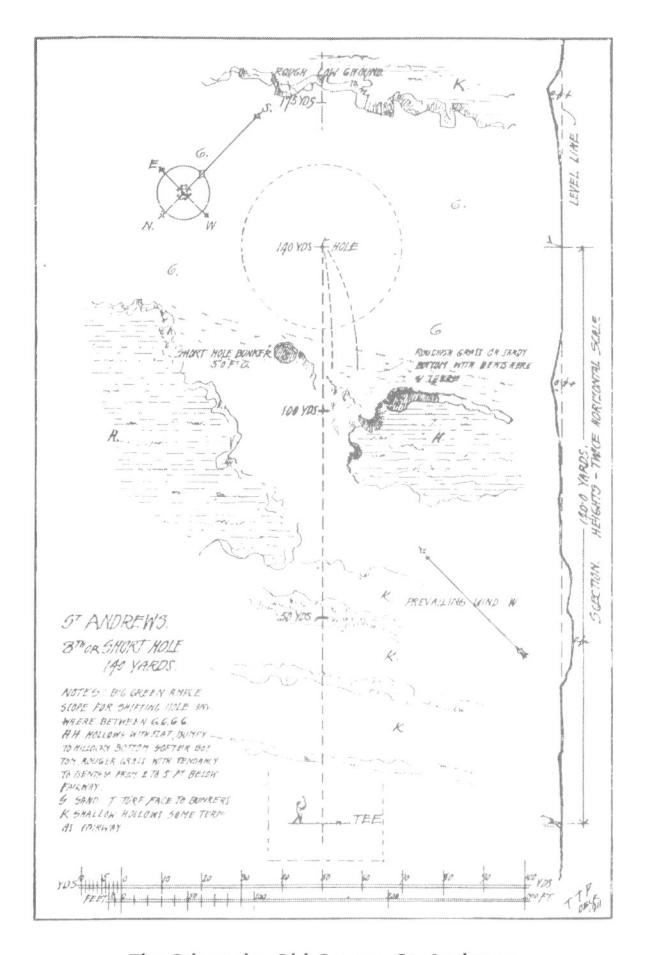

The 8th at the Old Course, St. Andrews

A 1911 rendering of the front nine's only par-3. Alister MacKenzie originally "despised" the hole. "It appears absurdly simple, but so far from familiarity breeding contempt, it has precisely the opposite effect. On medal play days the flag is usually placed behind the bunker and it is surprisingly difficult to get near it. A pitch over the bunker usually lands yards behind the hole. On the other hand, there is a ridge 100 yards from the tee on the right which runs diagonally towards the bunker. A well-played run up shot will climb this ridge, curl round the edge of the bunker and lie dead at the hole, but unless the ball has sufficient topspin to climb this ridge it will turn off at right angles and be deeply buried in the bunker to the left."

St. Andrews is difficult, not because bunkers are placed to catch inaccurate shots, but because the result of a misadventure is to make the next shot infinitely more difficult than it would otherwise have been.

H.N. WETHERED AND TOM SIMPSON

You must use something beside shots and clubs, playing St. Andrews. I can learn more in a week on that course than in a year on many a sterling championship test in America.

BOBBY JONES

St. Andrews is the least obvious course in the world. It is covered with concealed rolls, bunkers, hollows, and hummocks, which become more and more bewildering as the ground becomes harder.

BOBBY JONES

I do not know of a single example of a successful golf architect who is not enamored of the Old Course and the strategic principles embodied in it.

ALISTER MACKENZIE

The 11th Hole at St. Andrews
A 1911 survey of the Eden, Old Course at St. Andrews.

Bernard Darwin wrote that "the only consoling thing about the hole is that the green slopes upward, so that it is not quite so easy for the ball to run over it as it otherwise would be. This is really but cold comfort, however, because the danger of going too far is not so imminent as that of not going straight enough. There is one bunker called 'Strath,' which is to the right, and there is another called the 'Shelly Bunker,' to the left; there is also another bunker short of Strath to catch the thoroughly short and ineffective ball. The hole is as a rule cut fairly close to Strath, wherefore it behoves the careful man to play well away to the left, and not to take undue risks by going straight for the hole.

"This may sound pusillanimous, but trouble once begun at this hole may never come to an end till the card is torn into a thousand fragments."— Golfing great Harold Hilton gave the Eden considerable thought.

"When I first played the short eleventh hole at St. Andrews, I thought it was a simple looking hole, and I played it as if that really were the case. But I have had, indeed, good reason to come to the conclusion that my initial success in the playing of this hole was mainly due to ignorance in regard to its difficulty. That wretched 'Strath' bunker on the right has claimed my ball many, many times—far oftener, in fact, than any other hazards I have come across."

Then Hilton summed up the beauty of options in design, particularly when it comes to searching for ways to challenge a player of his caliber.

"Whenever I come to play this particular hole I always wish I were temporarily suffering from a loss of memory, so that I could tackle it without any sad recollections of the past. It is a simple looking hole to look at, but it is such a difficult one to play. It may be that it is difficult by virtue of the fact that there are so many ways in which it can be played that one cannot quite arrive at a definite conclusion as to which is the most advisable."

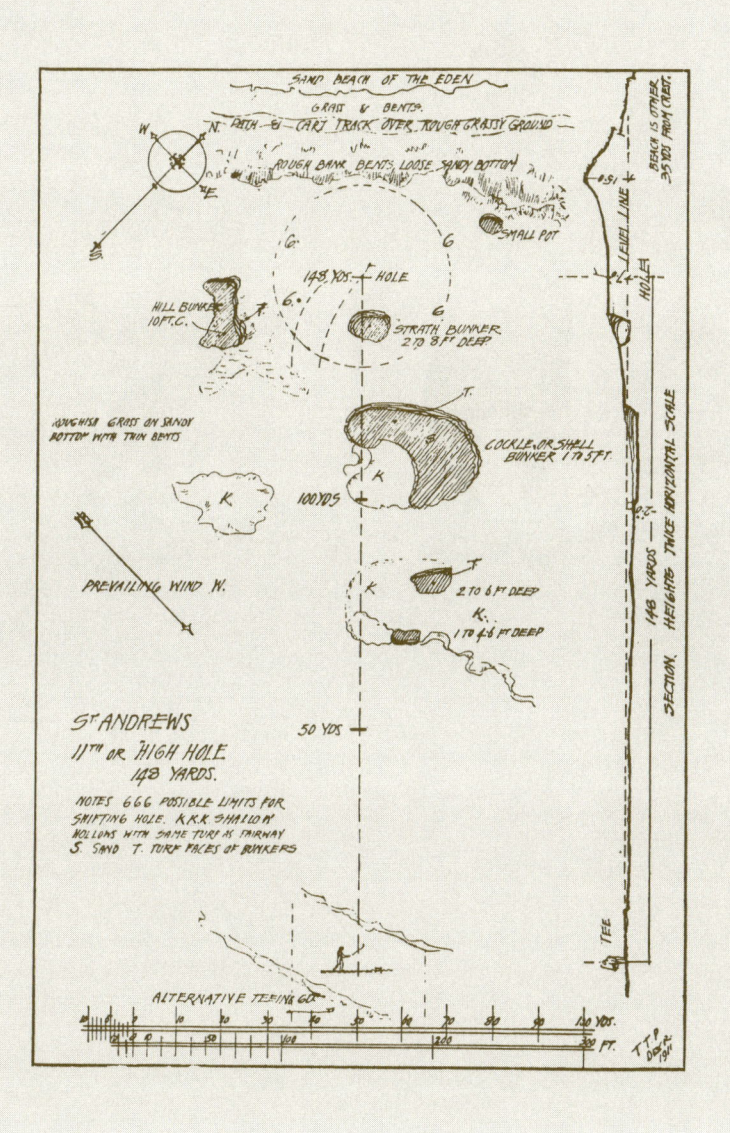

Pompus Player (who fancies his golf): "And what do I take for this carry?"
Old Dick (who doesn't): "Lemme see, Var-r-don took a mashie, Br-r-aid a half-iron, Taylor a mashie. Tak' yer driver, an' play shor-r-t."

LINKS

The British Isles were covered by glaciers fifteen thousand years ago. As those glaciers melted, the turbulent sea levels rose and fell, depositing sand along the immediate coastlines.

Over the last six centuries these sandy areas were further exposed as sea levels dropped. Wind-whipped dunes were formed, covered by plant material and bent grasses seeded via bird droppings. These coastline dune systems went untouched by the nearby farmers who wanted no part of the porous, nutrient-depleted soil. But rabbits gladly claimed these odd landscapes.

With golf at St. Andrews and Prestwick becoming more popular, towns looked to late nineteenth-century golf professionals to route courses over these odd seaside grounds.

"Nature was their architect, and beast and man her contractors," Sir Guy Campbell wrote of early links courses.

The rabbits became admired for their ability to maintain the natural bent grasses. Architect Alister MacKenzie praised the rabbits for their ability to create "sparse, dwarf, velvety" turf where balls sat up in a "remarkable manner." Eventually, the rabbits multiplied too rapidly for some and were replaced by mowers and fertilizers. Even so, Alister MacKenzie insisted years later that humans never managed the turf as well (see the Upkeep chapter, p. 83 for more on this).

Dictionaries suggest multiple origins for the term "links." The early Scottish word "lynkis" means "ridges and hummocks or open rough ground," while C.B. Macdonald provided a links definition in *Scotland's*

Gift—Golf, describing links as the "windings of a river" or the "rich ground lying among" the windings. An ancient Oxford definition suggests that "links" is an old English derivation of "hlinc," defined as "lean." Perhaps not coincidentally, the idea of leanness suggests the turfgrass characteristic most vital to fast, firm links golf.

Beyond semantics, the playing characteristics of linksland must meet certain requirements for a links to earn its certificate of authenticity. Robert Hunter referred to "those crumpled and corrugated areas" distinguished by intense fairway undulations that induce bounces both good and bad, but rarely anything in between."

"The undulations possess the contours suggestive of motion, inviting the run of the ball over the variable slopes," wrote H.N. Wethered, noted author and collaborator with Tom Simpson on *The Architectural Side of Golf*. "The true links have an intimacy with the waves; they are much on the same level, in close relation, almost cousins and part of the ocean if you can imagine sea turned into land or the land suffering sea change into something rich and rare."

After all, Wethered wrote, "the wind is answerable for the foaming undulations of the seas as it is for the thin borderlands of the links. It is indeed not inappropriate to regard the greens as worthy symbols of the bluer undulations beyond."

■

The true links were molded by divine hands. Linksland, the fine grasses, the wind-made bunkers that defy imitation, the exquisite contours that refuse to be sculptured by hand—all these were given lavishly by a divine dispensation to the British.

ROBERT HUNTER

The Nature the golf architect has in mind is linksland upon which golf has been played for hundreds of years, and remained through a major part of this time uncontaminated by the hand of man except for the cutting of the holes. Whatever beauty such land possessed was inherent in it, and those today who have played golf amidst such primeval surroundings are conscious of a certain charm wholly lacking upon a palpable man-made golf course.

MAX BEHR

The charm of the seaside courses of Great Britain lies in their multiformity, their unconventionality, their infinite variety. There are eighteen holes, and the yardage is up to standard, but comparison largely ends there. The terrain itself has an individuality all its own. In its uneven diversity, its tumbling irregularity, its unrivalled originality, linksland bears no resemblance to any other territory.

ROBERT HUNTER

A hazardless golf links is Hamlet without the Prince of Denmark, or whisky and soda without the whisky. It is insipid and uneventful, that is, it is not a golf links.

HORACE HUTCHINSON

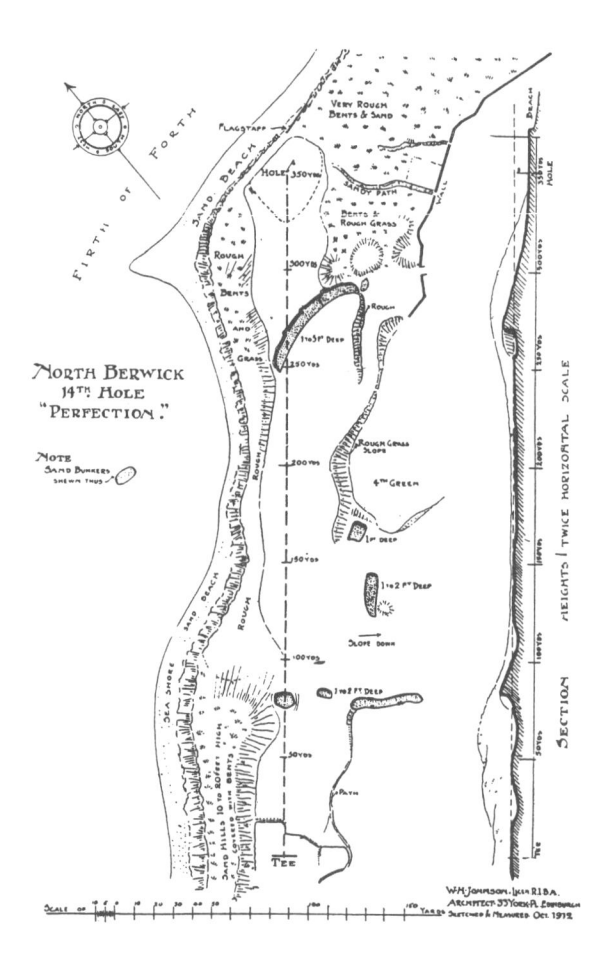

North Berwick West's Perfection

Bernard Darwin wrote that even though North Berwick "is no longer short, it is still an exceptionally good school in which to learn the art of approaching." Darwin's "considerable respect" for the course was "born of fear and conscious incompetence," and extended "towards a course where the ground is a little hard and bumpy."

Of the par-4 14th, Perfection, Darwin writes that "with the tee shot we must hug as closely as we dare the side of a big hill on the left, and if we fall into the opposite extreme, we may slice our ball among the rocks of 'Carl Kemp.' All being well, we have a reasonably easy second over a bunker; but we cannot see where we are going, and have the uncanny feeling that we are hitting straight into the sea."

The golf holes on the best links in Scotland and England have several different ways of playing them, and because they do not present just one and only one way to everybody, the interest in the game increases with the diversity of its problems.

DONALD ROSS

The difference between the golf courses of America and of Great Britain can best be expressed by the two words "artificial" and "natural": and that means a whole lot more than the mere presence or absence of the fabrication of man ... Employing a comparison with our own best courses in America I have found that most of our courses, especially those inland, may be played correctly the same way round after round. The holes really are laid out scientifically; visibility is stressed; you can see what you have to do virtually all the time; and when once you learn how to do it, you can go right ahead, the next day, and the next day, and the day after that.

BOBBY JONES

So goes golf on the links—those sacred bits of God's earth—where men have battled for generations, like the sailor or the mountaineer, with what nature has placed before them.

ROBERT HUNTER

Portrait of a gentleman arriving on the 18th green

■ HOW the GAME TORMENTS the ADVENTUROUS SOUL ■

"How the game torments the adventurous soul."

Yet another immortal line from that enduring writing duet, Wethered and Simpson, and their 1929 tome, *The Architectual Side of Golf*.

Or was it Robert Hunter who originated the phrase in 1926?

"How the game torments the adventurous soul, even him who with a bit of rag and a hollow shell defies wind and wave!" Hunter wrote. "Golf beats us all, and that is the chief reason we shall never cease loving her, nor ever give up our attempt to subdue her."

The difference between adventure and difficulty proved to be a delicate concept for the old architects. They were hoping to arouse the golfer's mind and capture his heart without crushing his soul.

The architects never wanted the game to be dull, but they also never intended to create something so punishing that the golfer lost his appetite for adventure. The fine line between an exciting activity and agony explains their emphasis on courses that presented options as much as they tested the ability to hit shots.

The master designers saw this as the most important battle they could wage for the future of golf, and of course, they were correct in their fears that courses would eventually seek to overvalue the ability to hit the ball on a straight line to the hole. These "penal" golf courses do not contribute to, as Max Behr said, "the amenities of life," instead contributing only to life's "trials and tribulations." And as Alister MacKenzie pointed out, for the golfer reconciled to playing a penal course, "the time inevitably comes when he gets tired of golf, without knowing the reason why."

We all know the golfer who seems to enjoy the beating inflicted by a Pine Valley or an Oakmont. Both are penal courses on first glance, but clearly full of strategic options after repeat visits.

Writer Bernard Darwin recounted the torment that he and a golfing friend felt after going round the maddeningly quirky Old Course which Darwin said did "worse than punish a man; it makes him ridiculous."

"There was an American friend of mine," Darwin wrote. "He was a new member of the Royal and Ancient Club and this was his first visit, but he had read and heard so much beforehand that he could tell the name of every bunker even as his ball was speeding toward it for the first time. He had only one gentle complaint, he had been there for nearly a week and with only one round left to play he had never yet been into Strath, perhaps the most famou—or infamous—bunker of them all.

"His unspoken prayer was answered and with the last tee shot to the eleventh hole in he went, and, what was more, his ball lay impossibly tucked up under the overhanging brink, so that he could scarcely stand or play his club. With a radiant countenance he plunged in after it and it was only with his fifth thump that he got out. Then he felt for the first time that he had won his spurs and been given the freedom of the Old Course.

"He and I came away from St. Andrews together and sat for some time on my bed in the sleeping car talking it all over again. There were many other golfers on that train and there was not one of us, I suppose, who had not in the last day or two called Gods and men to witness that the course was grossly unfair. Neither was there one of us that two minutes later had not been analyzing yet again the surpassing greatness of it—the most damnable and infinitely the most lovable links in the world."

Courses have no doubt been getting more and more difficult for the average player. His golf has in some cases been a dismal progress from the rough to a bunker, and from a bunker to the rough, hole after hole. He has very likely chosen a pleasant spring day for a little relaxation and pleasure, and returns to his home at night in a jaded and almost hopeless frame of mind.

H.S. COLT

What is more engaging than to see how golf infuriates some big brute who can thrash anybody, ride bucking horses, shoot deer on the run and birds on the wing! What is so delectable as to see him in a nervous tremor as he stands on the tee, glaring fiercely at that still, white, little ball! How the game torments the adventurous soul …

TOM SIMPSON AND H.N. WETHERED

It is a remarkable thing about golf courses that nearly every man has an affection for the particular mud heap on which he plays. It is probably largely due to associations: his friends play there, he knows the course and can probably do a lower score than elsewhere. He may perhaps also have pleasant recollections of the dollars he has won from his opponents. It may not be a real course at all. There may be no interest or strategy about it; it simply gives an opportunity for exercise and "socking" a golf ball. He is opposed to any alterations being made to it, but the time inevitably comes when he gets tired of golf, without knowing the reason why. Perhaps after spending a holiday on some good golf course he clamors for the reconstruction of his home course, or migrates elsewhere.

ALISTER MACKENZIE

The only course that will remain difficult under all conditions will be one that is designed and kept for golf of a stereotyped, monotonous character, and this makes a most uninteresting proposition.

BOBBY JONES

It is not the love of something easy which has drawn men like a magnet for hundreds of years to this royal and ancient pastime; on the contrary, it is the maddening difficulty of it.

ROBERT HUNTER

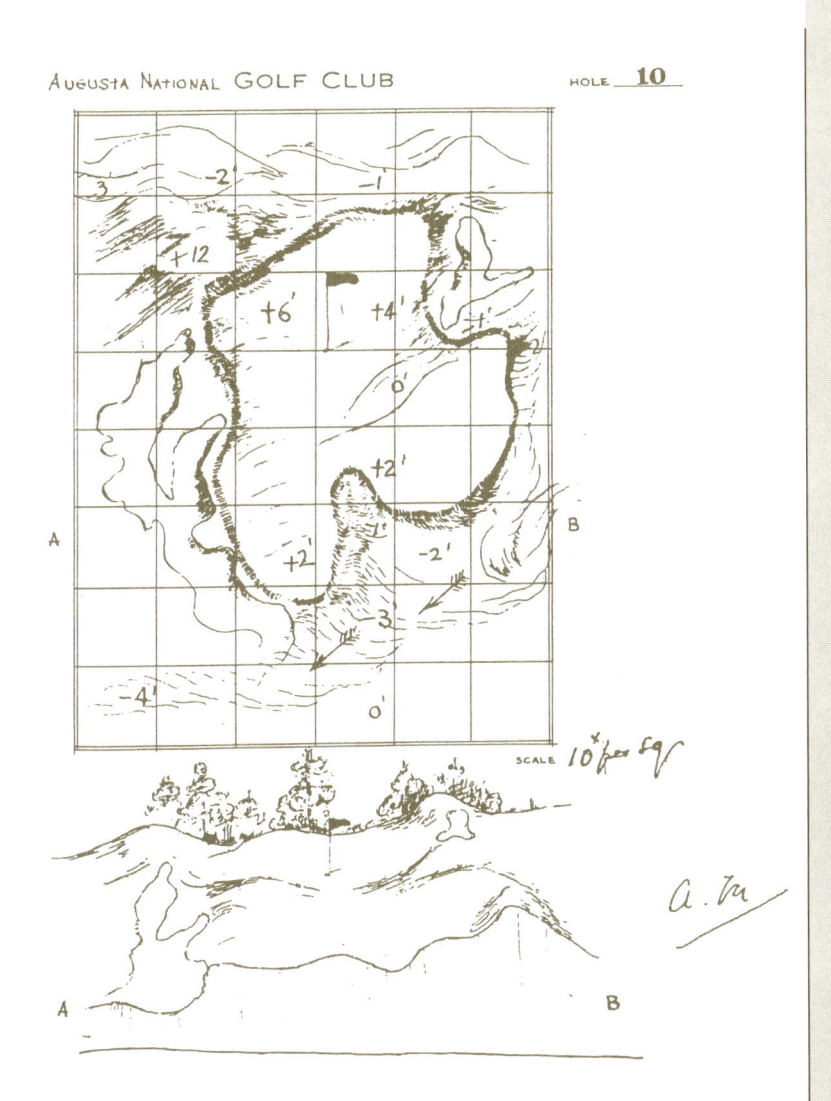

MacKenzie's First at Augusta National

Of Alister MacKenzie's green renderings for Augusta National, his original 10th hole sketch (today's first hole) differs most significantly from the green that was actually built. While his other renderings appear close to the final product, the green was eventually built without both greenside bunkers depicted here. A fronting hazard was later added.

William Langford and Strategy

Architect William Langford practiced throughout the Midwest during the later years of the Golden Age. His courses were often mistaken for Seth Raynor designs because he employed a similar style of deep-faced bunkering and bold green contours.

In a short essay titled "Placing Hazards," Langford demonstrates two ways to employ strategic design. Figure 2 "shows five ways of playing the same hole, at least one of which is well within the ability of any golfer. The echelon arrangement of bunkers for the tee shot allows three carries of widely varying length. The second shot bunkers are placed so as to offer a reward proportionate to the risk taken at the tee. Figure 3 shows a hole with two avenues of play, one for the short driver, one for the long. He who chooses the short carry from the tee is confronted with a very difficult second to the green; he who successfully negotiates the long carry is rewarded by an open approach."

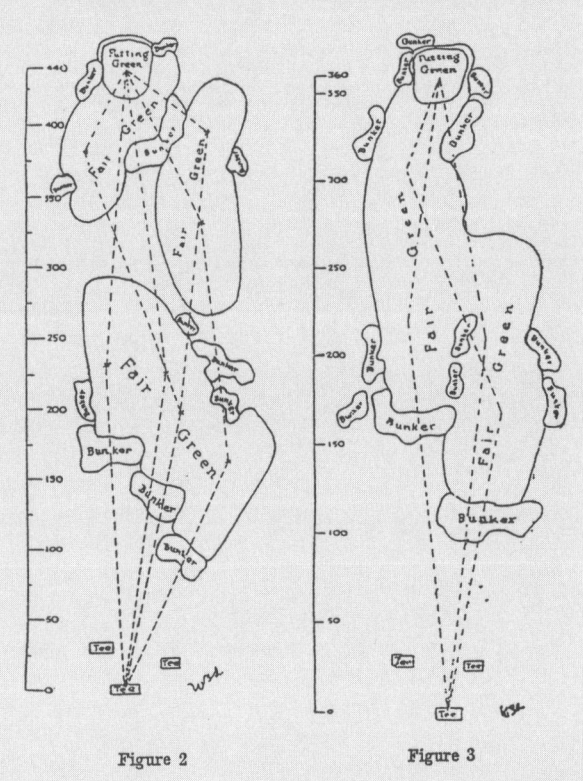

Figure 2   Figure 3

Golf architecture, because it is an art, has to do with furthering the amenities of life. But when so-called architecture only contributes to its trials and tribulations, it loses both the sense and the dignity of its calling.

MAX BEHR

Golf is an effort to do a very delicate thing with implements ill adapted to the purpose, which is the reason golfers are constantly endeavoring to improve their game by trying out different clubs and different ways of hitting the ball; and practicing constantly.

GEORGE C. THOMAS JR.

Searching for a lost ball is not a pleasant vocation, but since golf was first played a lost ball has always been a part of the game. So reconcile yourself to tradition.

C.B. MACDONALD

On the golf course a man may be the dogged victim of inexorable fate, be struck down by an appalling stroke of tragedy, become the hero of unbelievable melodrama, or the clown in a side-splitting comedy.

BOBBY JONES

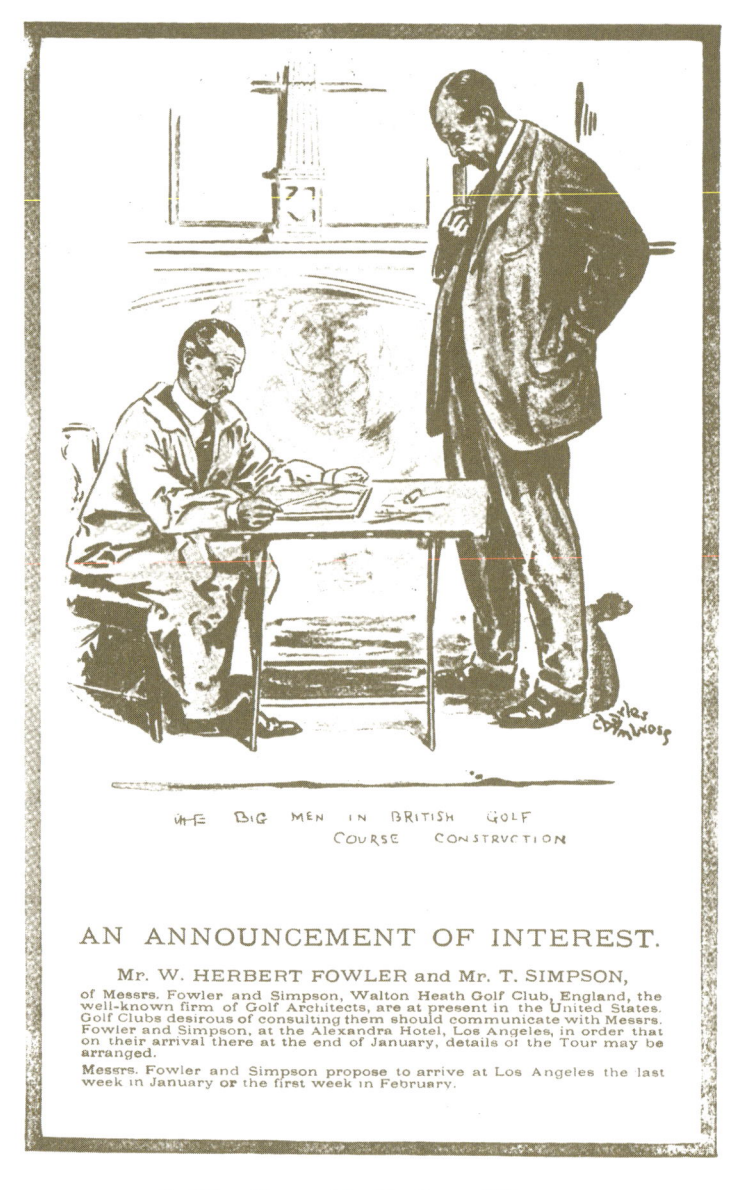

THE BIG MEN IN BRITISH GOLF
COURSE CONSTRUCTION

AN ANNOUNCEMENT OF INTEREST.

Mr. W. HERBERT FOWLER and Mr. T. SIMPSON,

of Messrs. Fowler and Simpson, Walton Heath Golf Club, England, the well-known firm of Golf Architects, are at present in the United States. Golf Clubs desirous of consulting them should communicate with Messrs. Fowler and Simpson, at the Alexandra Hotel, Los Angeles, in order that on their arrival there at the end of January, details of the Tour may be arranged.

Messrs. Fowler and Simpson propose to arrive at Los Angeles the last week in January or the first week in February.

An Advertisement for Fowler and Simpson
Ads and articles announcing pending architect visits were quite common in the 1920s.

The ARCHITECT

"No man can be a good architect unless he has a wide experience of many courses, a most observant eye for the weaknesses of his brother golfers, and red-hot zeal for his art, so that he is more interested in seeing other people play holes than in playing them himself," wrote Bernard Darwin.

The master writer loved architecture and the Old Course. He kindly introduced several architects to his readership and made a habit of visiting courses under construction in hopes of learning more about the curious new profession of the "golf architect." Later in his career, Darwin shared his insights into the role of the architect as both a planner and redesign specialist.

"I have at different times spent very interesting days with eminent architects upon the sites of their labours when those labours had scarcely begun—with Mr. Colt at Stoke Poges and St. George's Hill, with the late Mr. Abercromby at Coombe Hill and Addington. I have called those days interesting; I should have said awe-inspiring, so bewildered was my own state of mind, so lucid and determined was that of my companion.

"I would be shown a thicket so dense that we had to struggle through it with a motion of men swimming, and be told that this was the line to the first hole. The line might, for all I knew, have just as well been in precisely the opposite direction. Yet I fancy that if two architects had been set to work, their instinct would have guided them to start through that particular thicket and no other.

"In such cases there is nothing for it but to reflect humbly that, after all, it is the architect's job, and that it is only natural that he should do it better than a mere casual student. Yet these confounded architects can sometimes put us to shame when we really do think that we are as good as they are.

"When Rye had to be altered, I was on a Sub-Committee to consider possible changes. We thought hard and long: we devised a scheme and then we got Mr. [Tom] Simpson to come and polish it up for us. We were particularly well pleased with our new first hole, and a very good hole I venture to say it is, but the humiliating part of the business was this, that Mr. Simpson had only to move half-a-dozen yards or so from the place we had designed for the green to find one obviously much better. We had pored over the site and he had not. Why had we not discovered that place that was plain for all to see, when it was pointed out? I do not know, and whatever I might admit on my own account I hesitate to say that all my companions were stupid. The fact remains that we had not. So must needs say, 'Hooroar for the architects.'

"I imagine this altering and remodeling of courses is in fact a more delicate and difficult task than that of laying out a new one. The architect has neither so free a hand nor such agreeable privacy; everybody can see what he is at and can criticize accordingly. Moreover, he is sure to find himself opposed to vested interests in the shape of holes that have long and often deservedly been regarded with love and veneration."

Just as one can see and appreciate beautiful paintings without being able himself to paint, so can one play and appreciate hundreds of golf courses without being able to develop that natural aptitude and artistic sense which, to my mind, contribute so largely to the successful and outstanding accomplishments of a golf architect.

CHARLES BANKS

The golf architect is undoubtedly by the stern necessity of his calling bound to be a "plotter"—that is to say, he has to contrive schemes (occasionally marked by a mildly devilish ingenuity) in order to control and govern a game which has several remarkable peculiarities of its own.

TOM SIMPSON AND H.N. WETHERED

■

An architect should never lose sight of his responsibility as an educational factor in the game. Nothing will tend more to develop the right spirit of the game than an insistence upon the high ideals that should inspire sound golf architecture. Every course needs not be a Pine Valley or a National, but every course should be so constructed as to afford incentive to and provide a reward for high-class play; and by high-class play is meant, simply the best of which each individual is himself capable.

WILLIAM FLYNN

■

An architect's earnest hope is, without doubt, that his courses will have the necessary vitality to resist possibly adverse criticism, and will endure as a lasting record of his craft and of his love for his work.

H.S. COLT

■

The average golfer is just about as competent to construct a golf course out of a rough tract of real estate as he is to plan an expensive house and build it, and the same may be said of the average golf professional. The same class of man is needed to build a course as is needed to build a clubhouse, except that he must be more imaginative with infinitely less written lore to guide him.

DEVEREUX EMMET

Some architects are faintly contemptuous of suggestions made by "amateurs," but the wise architect is aware that he does not know it all and that really good ideas are often developed in these conferences. He never turns down a sensible suggestion simply because it has been made by someone else. On the contrary he accepts it thankfully and promptly embodies it in his plans.

WILLIAM FLYNN

A good golf architect, like a good surgeon or a good financial advisor, must be thoroughly dependable at all times. Careful personal supervision is essential.

CHARLES BANKS

The principal consideration of the architect is to design his course in such a way as to hold the interest of the player from the first tee to the last green and to present the problems of the various holes in such a way that they register in the player's mind as he stands on the tee or on the fairway for the shot to the green.

WILLIAM FLYNN

A first-class architect attempts to give the impression that everything has been done by nature and nothing by himself, whereas a contractor tries to make as big a splash as possible and impress committees with the amount of labor and material he has put into the job.

ALISTER MACKENZIE

The golf course architect soon realizes how impossible it is to please everyone, and sifts quickly the chaff from the wheat in the matter of suggestions appertaining to his work.

H.S. COLT

Mental balance is a matter of exceedingly delicate adjustment; and the true object of every game worthy of the name is to apply a test of the most searching kind possible in order to distinguish the superiority of one player over another. Without such a test a game would be scarcely worth the effort. The golf architect for this reason is fully justified in refusing to give the golfer just the kind of shot he would normally prefer.

H.N. WETHERED AND TOM SIMPSON

Colt, Fowler, and Abercrombie

A depiction of architects H.S Colt, Herbert Fowler, and J.F Abercrombie discussing the elements of design. Included with this illustration was a note that in 1914, "the University of Illinois had just added to its curriculum a course on golf links construction. There was speculation that England might do the same and if so Colt or Fowler seemed to be likely candidates for a Professional Chair and Lectureship." The war likely ended any plans for the golf design curriculum, and Abercrombie would later join the firm of Fowler and Simpson.

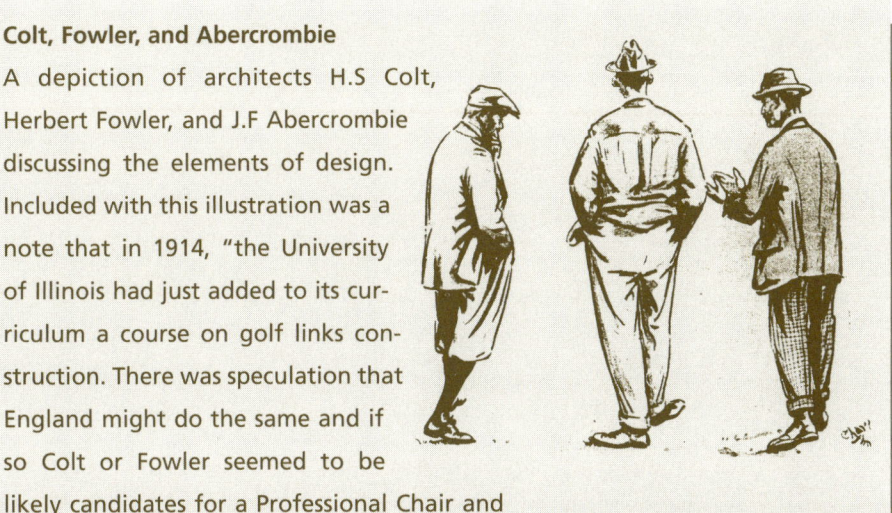

Colt displayed his sense of humor when taking on the subject of planning, as demonstrated by this memory:

"A leading man on the subject was introduced for the first time to 150 acres of good golfing ground, and we all gathered around to see the golf course created instantly. It was something like following a water-diviner with his twig of hazel. Without a moment's hesitation he fixed the first tee, and then, going away at full speed, he brought us up abruptly in a deep hollow, and a stake was set up to show the exact position of the first hole. Ground was selected for the second tee, and then we all started off again, and arrived in a panting state at a hollow deeper than the first, where another stake was set up for the second hole. Then away again at full speed for the third hole, and so on. Towards the end we had to tack backwards and forwards half a dozen times to get in the required number of holes. The thing was done in a few hours, lunch was eaten, and the train caught, but the course, thank heavens, was never constructed!"

Donald Ross
A drawing of architect Ross holding a plan for his most famous design commission, Pinehurst No. 2.

■

Some courses cannot safely put in a public appearance except on the darkest nights. Therefore, I believe it is safer, right at the beginning, to call in the specialist—the golf architect—and place on him the major responsibility for the designing and building of the course.

CHARLES BANKS

■

The golf architect is not at all concerned with chastising bad play. On the contrary, it is his business to arrange the field of play as to stimulate interest, and hence, the province of hazards is to chasten the too ambitious.

MAX BEHR

Don't be afraid to ask your architect questions, for if he is a true master of his craft he will not only welcome them but also discuss them. Surely I have had some queer theories advanced and some absurd suggestions have prompted a short answer. It is a bad habit and as I grow older I am trying to break it.

A.W. TILLINGHAST

What is "fair" for the one is regarded as the grossest injustice by the other. It falls to the lot, therefore, of the architect—in this case not always the happiest—to weigh the claims made on him as an impartial arbiter and to decide the issue according to the best of his judgment. He will not allow, if he can help it, the unduly powerful to terrorize the rest of the field with impunity, nor will he permit the weakest to go to the wall without a protest. In this laudable endeavor he is actuated by the best and most disinterested motives. His object is to encourage enthusiasm, mental agility and happiness in the hearts of all good golfers whether they be merely magnificent, passably good or totally indifferent. At the same time he must punish willful extravagance and ensure that the virtuous are rewarded.

TOM SIMPSON AND H.N. WETHERED

Utilizing Topography by Charles Banks

A few years ago, a golf club in the New York district found its course sadly in need of revision. This course had been in play only two seasons when a physician was called to come to diagnose its ailments. I happened to be the physician, and one glance at the patient convinced me that a major operation was necessary. The parents stood around with long faces and anxious expressions. As a golf committee, they had been responsible for bringing this sick baby into the world. They seemed to think, however, that the attending physician, or golf architect, was the really responsible person. "We placed full dependence upon him," said they in chorus.

On the sly, however, one member of the committee plucked me by the sleeve and drew me aside. "There's a history to this case," he whispered. "Want to hear it?"

"It might be helpful," I replied.

"Well," said he, "when we were ready to build this course, we began to look around for a golf architect. As you know one of the finest courses in the Metropolitan District is only a stone's throw from here. It looked good to us and we decided that we'd like to have a course like it. We learned who the architect was and had a talk with him. He named his fee and promptly asked for a topographical survey.

"How much will that cost?" we asked.

"Oh, in this case it will cost anywhere from eight hundred to one thousand dollars," he replied.

"Whew!" exclaimed some members of the committee. We thanked the architect for his advice, went into a huddle, and promptly arranged to see another architect.

"What would be your fee for this job?" we asked. He named a figure considerably lower than the first man. Some members of the committee raised

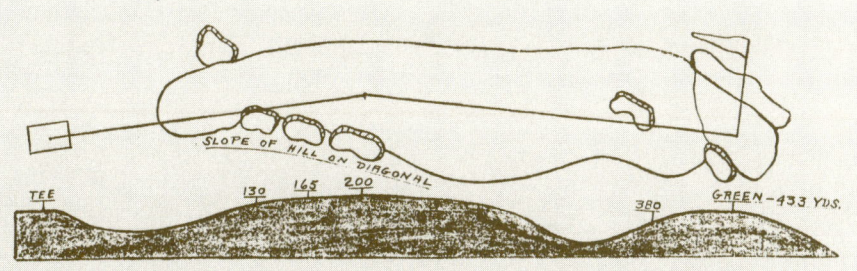

The plan and a cross section of the 8th hole at Castle Harbour in Bermuda

their eyebrows and nodded at each other, as much as to say, "This looks better. It sounds more like it."

"Would you require a topographical survey?" enquired a member of the committee.

"Topographical survey?" questioned the architect, with a sarcastic smile on his face. "Why that would just be a waste of money—eight hundred or a thousand dollars thrown away."

"Now the members of the committee looked at each other knowingly, as much as to say, "Didn't I tell you so?"

"The committee then went into another huddle and promptly, against my protest, voted to employ the second architect. At the time I said, "Look here, boys, the difference between these two men is that one plays by note and the other plays by ear, and you are voting for the one that plays by ear." And, continued he, "that is the reason why we have you out here today."

By a strange coincidence it happened that the architect who was rejected was the late Seth J. Raynor, the man with whom I had been associated before his death. And here was the committee, in a dilemma, calling on me for help after two seasons of play on a course which had been badly bungled because of a desire to save the expense of a topographical map and a slight additional amount in the architect's fee.

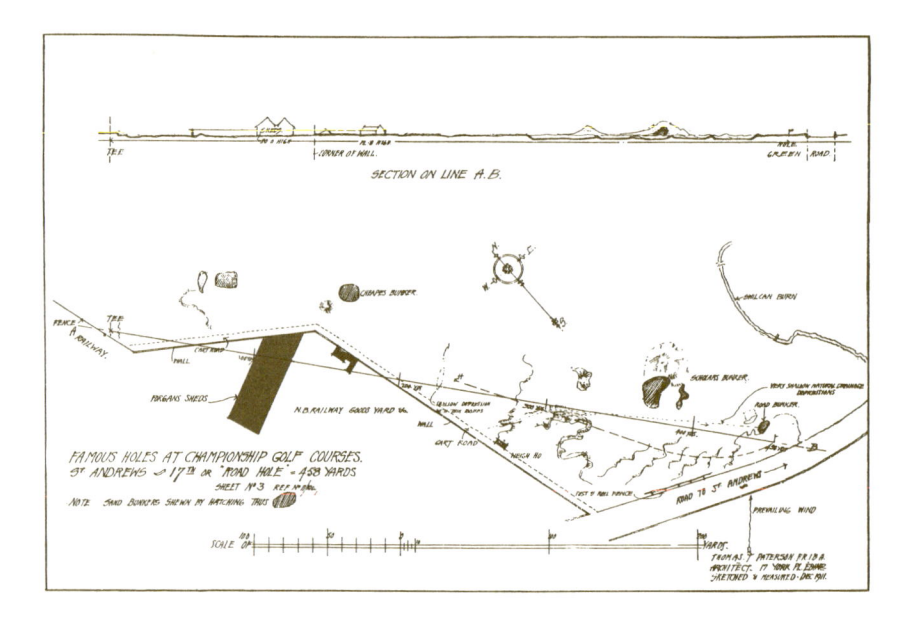

A Survey of the Road Hole

No hole defies conformity more than the 17th at St. Andrews. Local knowledge is rewarded, though some might argue that the better you know this hole and its many pitfalls, the harder it becomes to play.

STANDARDIZATION and LOCAL KNOWLEDGE

Nothing irritated the master architects more than attempts to standardize golf architecture. Whether committees were attempting to reach "accepted" yardages for various par designations or efforts were made to eliminate an advantage gained through local knowledge, the Golden Age designers knew from their days at St. Andrews that standardization would lead to architectural homogenization.

In his book *A Game of Golf*, the great amateur and 1913 U.S. Open champion Francis Ouimet recounted a story from the 1923 Walker Cup. It is just the kind of pro-local knowledge, anti-standardization story that warmed the heart of a MacKenzie or Tillinghast.

The tale naturally involved the Old Course. Where else but the home of local knowledge?

Ouimet was one down to the great Roger Wethered, son of H.N. Wethered and brother of the female golfing great Joyce Wethered.

"Then we came to the terrible seventeenth," Ouimet wrote of his match as it reached the Road hole. "This is a par five, but, like the fourteenth, reachable in two. The fact that you can get home in two does not mean a thing, because there are so many dangers trying for the green that it is hardly worth the effort. We had two good tee shots. I played an iron, a safety-first sort of stroke, that could get me to the front edge and no farther. That is where my ball ended.

"Wethered, who knew the St. Andrews course like a book, deliberately played to the left beyond the little trap guarding the green and onto the eighteenth tee. I did not understand why he should do such a thing, but it did not take me long to find out his reason. When we arrived at our balls, I was left with a nasty approach putt over a steep incline, a shot I abhor, whereas Roger had a nice place from which to roll his ball to the hole with nothing dangerous in the way. I putted and put my ball eight to ten inches from the cup. Wethered putted from off the green, got inside and that hole was halved."

Ouimet describes two totally different ways to play a par-5, a three-shotter reachable in two for most (and subsequently changed to a par-4 years later). And best of all, the green is guarded by a road, yet local knowledge offered more than one way to avoid bringing the road into play.

No wonder the architects fought so passionately against standardization.

■

… the sauce of golf is its variety. When you hear this wiseacre and that saying that there ought to be no cross bunkers, another that there ought to be no running-up shots, and so on, you may know at once they must all be wrong. Such words as "none'" and "all" should not appear in the laws laid down, for these matters. We want a little of each—"two pen'orth of all sorts," like the cabman's morning drink—some lofting approaches, some run-up and so on with the rest of the puzzles."

HORACE HUTCHINSON

Teeing Grounds for Two-Shot Holes

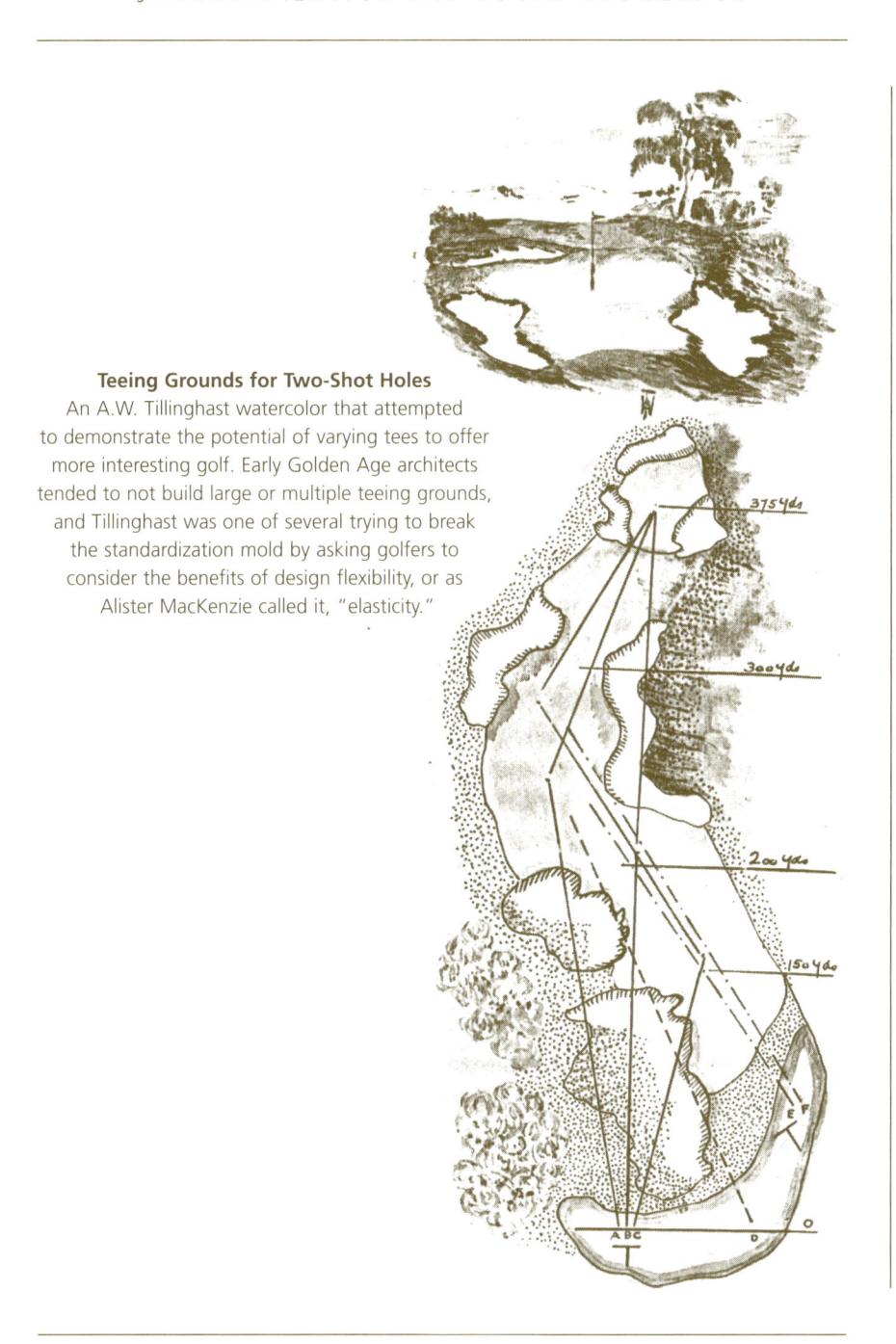

An A.W. Tillinghast watercolor that attempted to demonstrate the potential of varying tees to offer more interesting golf. Early Golden Age architects tended to not build large or multiple teeing grounds, and Tillinghast was one of several trying to break the standardization mold by asking golfers to consider the benefits of design flexibility, or as Alister MacKenzie called it, "elasticity."

Do not let certain standards become an obsession. Quality, not length; interest, not the number of holes; distinction, not the size in the greens—these things are worth striving for.

ROBERT HUNTER

… golf is a game and not a mathematical business, and … it is of vital importance to avoid anything that tends to make the game simple and stereotyped. On the contrary, every endeavor should be made to increase its strategy, variety, mystery, charm and elusiveness so that we shall never get bored with it, but continue to pursue it with increasing zest, as many of the old stalwarts of St. Andrews do, for the remainder of our lives.

ALISTER MACKENZIE

Don't worry about par. The practice of printing par figures is literally a mental hazard.

BOBBY JONES

The merit of any hole is not judged by its length but rather by its interest and its variety as elective play is apparent. It isn't how far but how good!

A.W. TILLINGHAST

A Tillinghast Sketch of San Francisco Golf Club Hole

Tillinghast described this "three-way" hole in a *Golf Illustrated* article.

"The green is undulating, with a pronounced flare working into the right front entrance. It is built up by scooping back the soil from in front, thus making a natural-looking dip and causing the green itself to stand up well from rather flat and featureless surroundings. The contours and placement of hazards render the green almost unassailable with a long shot from the right. It shows its best face to the second shot, a long iron or brassie coming directly in after the drive has made the long carry of the elbowing pits on the left. This, of course, is the true way to get par figures if there is power enough and courage back of the shots. Then there is the way around to the right, but this safe route gives the player absolutely no encouragement of getting home with any kind of a second, and consequently he is forced to play to the left before getting in to the green with the third. But there is still a third choice. By playing a very accurate and controlled drive to the left to that portion of the fairway which lies between the pits, the clear way to the green is opened up but it will take a tremendously long second to get home or into the swale in front. The sketch shows, by dotted lines, the three routes, and it is a matter of choice to be guided by a knowledge of the player's powers."

Immediately when we attempt to standardize sizes, shapes, and distances we lose more than half the pleasure of the game.

H.S. COLT

No real lover of golf with artistic understanding would undertake to measure the quality or fascination of a golf hole by a yard-stick, any more than a critic of poetry would attempt to measure the supreme sentiment expressed in a poem by the same method. One can understand the meter, but one cannot measure the soul expressed. It is absolutely inconceivable.

C.B. MACDONALD

It is the feel of the shots rather than the measure of tape that is the greatest asset to the builder of courses.

A.W. TILLINGHAST

So many people preach equity in golf. Nothing is so foreign to the truth. Does any human being receive what he conceives as equity in his life? He has got to take the bitter with the sweet, and as he forges through all the intricacies and inequalities which life presents, he proves his mettle. In golf the cardinal rules are arbitrary and not founded on eternal justice. Equity has nothing to do with the game itself.

C.B. MACDONALD

… it must be kept in mind that the elusive charm of the game suffers as soon as any successful method of standardization is allowed to creep in. A golf course should never pretend to be, nor is it intended to be, an infallible tribunal.

TOM SIMPSON AND H.N. WETHERED

The stretching out of holes to their last limit has often not only an evil effect on individual holes, but also on the layout in general and on the interest and quality of the course. It is refreshing now and then to find a club which has ignored the race for length and gone in for quality.

ROBERT HUNTER

It is has often been suggested that an uninteresting hole might be improved by lengthening it, but it would be a safe axiom to adopt, "It will only be made worse and take longer to play. Shorten it and get it over."

ALISTER MACKENZIE

A.W. Tillinghast
This H. Hymer drawing of Tillinghast appeared
in the August 1922 *Golf Illustrated*.

PLANNING and CONSTRUCTION

A.W. Tillinghast took on the less intriguing topics of planning and construction with grace. He also had a monthly column to fill in *Golf Illustrated,* which in those days was edited by Max Behr. Since Behr was a prominent golfer and authority, the amount of space devoted to Tillinghast's writings gives the appearance that Behr was trying to boost the career of the then up-and-coming Tillinghast.

But the writings were not just a marketing ploy to promote his fledgling design business. Tillinghast obviously had something to say when he wasn't in front of his piano, painting, or playing stellar golf. His many articles have since been lovingly compiled in three volumes that stand with any of the great books on the subject. Tillinghast never compiled a book on course design during his lifetime, but did have two works of fiction published, *The Mutt* and *Cobble Valley Golf Yarns.*

Introducing those two reproductions many years later, former USGA Executive Director Frank Hannigan speculated as to where the eccentric Tillinghast would fit in to today's golf architecture world.

"So how do you think A.W. Tillinghast would make out if we could have him disinterred, reborn and thrust into the competitive golf course architectural racket of the 1990s?" Hannigan wrote.

> **MODERN GOLF ARCHITECTURE**
> RECONSTRUCTION AND HAZARD CREATION
> WRITE FOR ILLUSTRATED BOOKLET
> **A·W·TILLINGHAST**
> 25 W·45 ST·   NEW YORK CITY
> *and*
> MUTUAL LIFE BUILDING
> PHILADELPHIA
> LILLIPUT LINKS *"miniatures"*

"I have no doubt how he'd do. Tillinghast would be the first full-time architect to have his own Gulfstream IV jet; his clients would include the Sultan of Brunei; he would own French vineyards and he would be proclaimed as the world's greatest architect—in his own advertising. In fact, the more I see of modern golf course architecture the more I revere Tillinghast and his primary rivals of the Golden Age of golf course architecture—Donald Ross, Alister MacKenzie, Seth Raynor, and William Flynn.

"He was the first architect who marketed himself. The famous handle-bar mustache was an integral part of the deal. So was the chauffeured limo in which he commuted from his baronial home in New Jersey to his office on New York's 45th Street.

"Tillinghast's primary assets as an architect were his roving mind, rich imagination and sense of aesthetics. He believed in variety, the converse of the appalling modern trick of imposing on the property one or more gimmicks linked to the architect, e.g., railroad ties or 'collection' bunkers. He did not say, 'See, this is all about me.' Thus, Winged Foot is not recognizable as having been created by the same man who turned out Baltusrol.

"The more I think on it, the more it's apparent that Tillinghast would have been a colossus today. The moderns would have been plowed under by a competitor who would not have hesitated to successfully bribe the *Golf Digest* selection panel, who could write complete English sentences, and who possessed a sense of irony."

In golf construction art and utility meet; both are absolutely vital; one is utterly ruined without the other.

GEORGE C. THOMAS JR.

A round of golf should present eighteen inspirations—not necessarily thrills, for spectacular holes may be sadly overdone. Every hole may be constructed to provide charm without being obtrusive with it.

A.W. TILLINGHAST

A golf architect must approach each bit of country with an absolute open mind, with no preconceived ideas of what he is going to lay out; the holes have to be found, and the land in its natural state used to its best advantage. Nature can always beat the handiwork of man and to achieve the best and most satisfactory results in laying out a golf course, you must humor nature.

WILLIE PARK JR.

We must be allowed to ease the tension at occasional intervals for our sanity, so that our brains may cool and our hearts expand with renewed life and freedom.

TOM SIMPSON AND H.N. WETHERED

■

A badly routed and planned course can be improved, but it rarely can be made perfect. It is analogous to a bad fitting coat.

ALISTER MACKENZIE

■

Frequently the natives resent the invasion of the golf pioneer.... Once an irate farmer emptied a thirty-three at myself and the engineer at a range of only five hundred yards, and he made us take cover too. He was a renter, and knew that we were there for no good. As he took no interest whatever in the Royal and Ancient.

A.W. TILLINGHAST

■

God builds golf links and the less man meddles the better for all concerned.

HERBERT FOWLER

■

Building a golf course and then calling in a golf architect afterwards to remedy the defects is like "building" your own suit of clothes and then calling in a tailor to give them style and reinforce the seams so that they won't rip in vital spots. The way some golf courses rip after being built is appalling.

CHARLES BANKS

In planning a golf course there are no fixed rules to which it is compulsory to conform, and the variety which results is one of the greatest charms of the game.

C.H. ALISON

I know well two great champions of earlier years who cannot now always carry a hazard one hundred yards from the tee, but who still play the game and have shots in their bag which Hagen and Jones would view with envy. On my ideal course these shall not be denied nor yet humiliated.

ROBERT HUNTER

It is impossible in considering types of holes for a course to suggest any positive sequence of alignment, for each layout should be designed to fit the particular ground on which it lies.

WILLIAM FLYNN

It is practically impossible to lay out a golf links to best advantage by contract any more than a picture can be painted by contract.

DEVEREUX EMMET

LINES OF CHARM

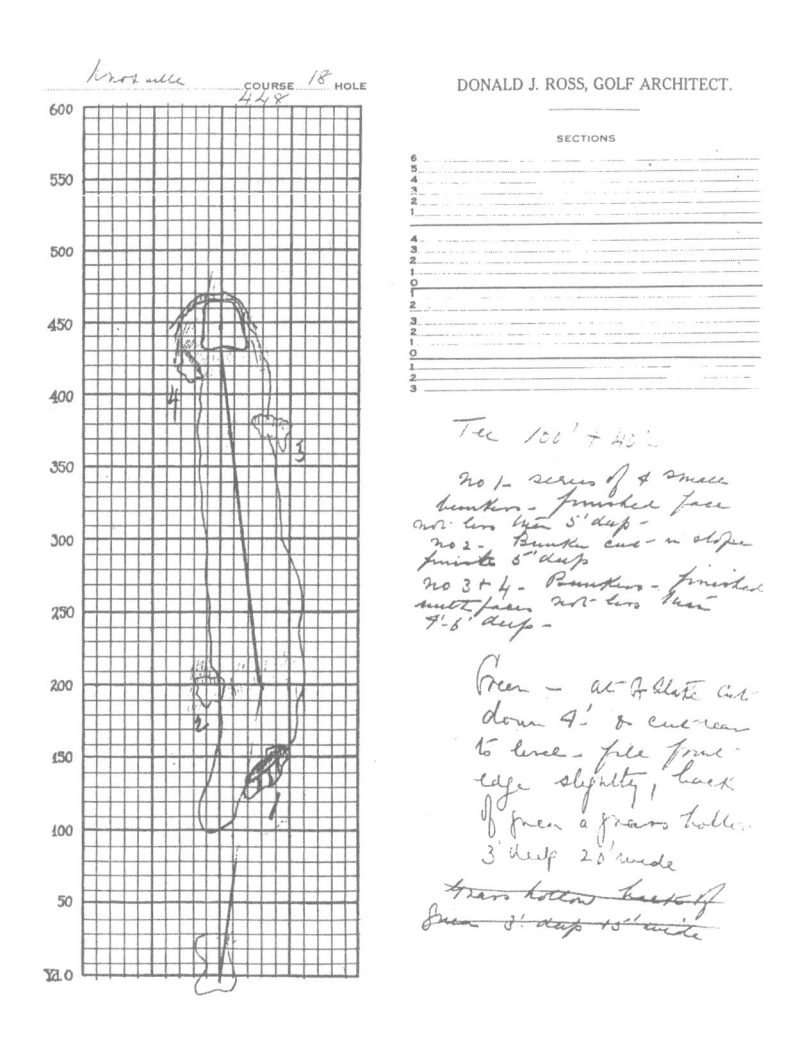

Donald Ross Field Sketch
A rarely seen Donald Ross field sketch for Holston Hills, in Tennessee.
The notes, in handwriting only a doctor could read, were directions
for his construction team.

It is my theory that nature must precede the architect in the laying out of links. It is futile to attempt the transformation of wholly inadequate acres into an adequate course. Invariably the result is the inauguration of an earthquake. The site of a golf course should be there, not brought there.

PERRY MAXWELL

Viewing the monstrosities created on many modern golf courses which are a travesty on Nature, no golfer can but shudder for the soul of golf. It would seem that in this striving after "novelty and innovation," many builders of golf courses believe they are elevating the game. But what a sad contemplation!

C.B. MACDONALD

It is far better to dig into the ten million golf holes which have never been built than to duplicate some of those which are almost as old as the game itself. Not that some of the ancient holes are not great. They are great where they already exist but how entirely out of place they are when nature does not cooperate. The hat which Madame gives the cook after wearing it a bit, seldom looks so well on the other's head.

A.W. TILLINGHAST

Fashions in golf courses, as in ladies' clothes, seem to be so frequently hopelessly exaggerated. We have our latest Parisian styles, and they are adopted for every form and every contour, quite regardless of the land to be dealt with.

H.S. COLT

Vitality is another quality that is essential. Instinctively we feel that one course is alive, another dead and insipid, lacking energy of expression. We look for the unexpected note and a pleasantness of line. Every curve should have a spring in it, and no straight line should ever be quite straight. Generally the detection of these slight differences is purely a matter of feeling which once experienced is not likely to be forgotten.

TOM SIMPSON AND H.N. WETHERED

The ultimate character of the course must be developed as the construction progresses.

WILLIAM FLYNN

■

The majority of American golf clubs are in the red, gore of the steam shovel, blood drawn by mound builders. We have learned nothing from Scotland and England where the ancient and honorable game can be enjoyed on marvelous links at one tenth the admission fees, dues, green fees, etc., that prevail in the land of the free.

PERRY MAXWELL

■

Often it is necessary to get from one section to another over ground which is not suited to the easiest construction, but that troublesome hole must be made to stand right up in meeting with the others, and if it has not got anything about that might make it respectable, it has got to have quality knocked into it until it can hold its head up in polite society.

A.W. TILLINGHAST

■

There has been a veritable debauch in golf links expenditure and it has got to stop. The world will be poor for a long time after this war. An old Scotch gentleman lately visited one of these ultra modern American golf courses of the most ultra expensive type, under construction. He looked it all over and then remarked sadly, "The game of gowf will no stand it."

DEVEREUX EMMET

■

Slopes, hills, mounds, or any other natural contour, which affect the roll or run of the ball, are aids on all parts of your fairways; and your strategy should, if possible, hinge on them. If you have no natural contours, you may build them. Compel your golfers to try for certain shots by these natural or artificial hazards, and teach them to play different types of strokes, and best of all, to place them.

GEORGE C. THOMAS JR.

■

Strive to retain as much of the natural ground formation as possible. The most beautiful courses are the ones that hew most closely to nature.

STANLEY THOMPSON

PLANNING AND CONSTRUCTION

Visitor: I see you have adopted the new method of
employing explosives for bunker formation.
Member: Oh no! That's only Major Blowhard
in the bunker at the 6th.

After the Drought
Golfer: "Well, greenkeeper, and what do you
think of *this* weather?"
Greenkeeper: Fine, sir—it's FINE!"

■ UPKEEP ■

*S*ince the practice of golf architecture was still a novel concept to early twentieth-century golfers, many of the architects focused their writings on essential design issues while avoiding the still foreign topic of course maintenance.

This does not mean they avoided the subject altogether.

Many of the architects longed for the days when rabbits maintained early links courses, with Alister MacKenzie going so far to say that fairway conditions at Machrihanish had "appreciably deteriorated" when rabbits no longer nibbled on the grass.

"The beautiful velvety turf as been replaced by rich agricultural grasses, daisies, and weeds," he wrote. "As the club accumulates more funds they are used to destroy the gorgeous natural features."

In later writings, it became apparent that the architects appreciated improved turfgrass conditions. Hugh and Alan Wilson, creators of Merion Cricket Club's two courses with help from future master architect William Flynn, devoted much of their spare time to developing better growing conditions. They worked closely with George Crump at Pine Valley, searching for ways to make grass grow on the pine barrens of New Jersey. Some even questioned the wisdom of building the course on soil so unsuited for golf. Thankfully, those critics were ignored.

Some architects feared that courses would become so well maintained that they'd lose some of the natural, "rub-of-the-green" seasoning that made every shot an adventure.

"I remember many years ago at Sunningdale," wrote MacKenzie, "a fussy, oily individual coming up to Harry Colt and saying, 'I really must congratulate you, Mr. Colt, on your fairways. They are perfect.' Colt, who objected to this type of man, answered somewhat testily, 'I don't agree with you at all.'"

"'Why not, Mr. Colt?' he asked.

"'The lies are too damned good,' was the answer."

After a course has been completed, it should have extra good care. Golf courses are like babies—they require a great deal of attention, especially in their early days. Upkeep that is properly provided for in the preliminary stages of the finished course is invaluable. Nothing later on can take its place.

CHARLES BANKS

If I had my way there would be a troupe of cavalry horses running though every trap and bunker on the course before a tournament started, where only a niblick could get the ball out and then but only a few yards. I have seen a number of traps and bunkers that afforded better lies and easier strokes than the fairway. This, of course, is ridiculous.

C.B. MACDONALD

The Home Hole at the National Golf Links of America,
Illustrated by Franklin Booth

■

If we have never had a bad lie we are not likely to appreciate a good one, moreover, the ability to play from a bad lie differentiates between a good player and a bad one. We might also remark that good and bad lies differentiate between good sportsmen and bad.

ALISTER MACKENZIE

■

Any idea that the upkeep of a course is a simple matter has probably by now been dissipated.

TOM SIMPSON AND H.N. WETHERED

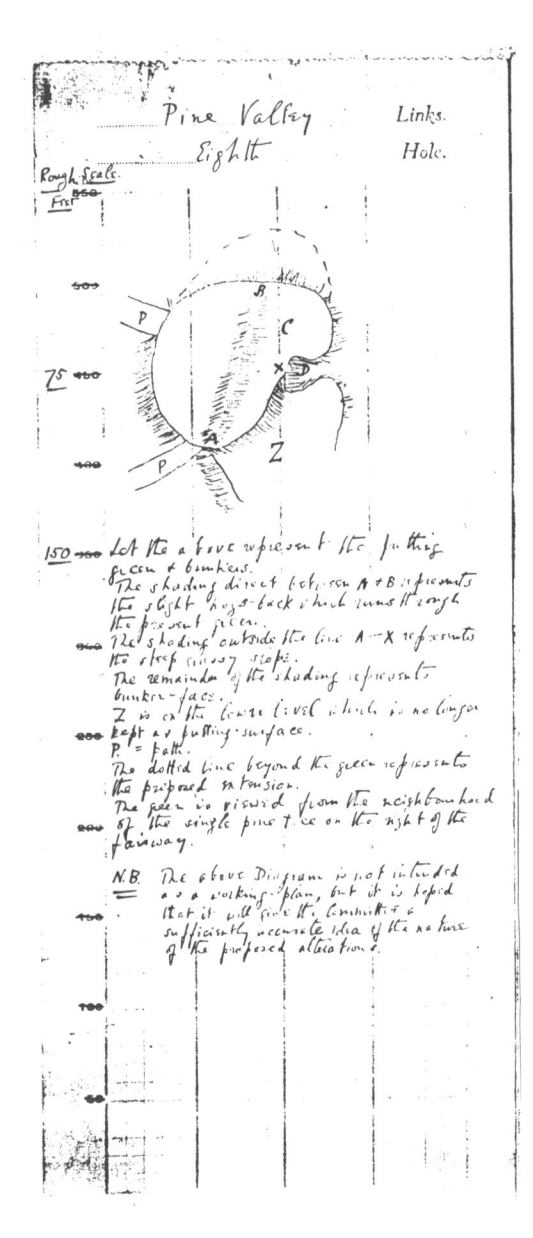

C.H. Alison's Plan for No. 8 at Pine Valley

Around 1920, architect C.H. Alison was asked to analyze George Crump's Pine Valley design. The longtime partner of H.S. Colt, who consulted Crump on the original design, Alison praised the course but did suggest enhancements to several greens. This is his plan for changes to the short par-4 eighth green.

A principle never to be lost sight of, in the construction as well as in the upkeep of a golf course, is this: no matter where the ball comes to rest a player should have a chance to swing the club and to hit the ball.

ROBERT HUNTER

All bunkers should have a rough, broken, uneven edge which gives the effect of coast erosion.

TOM SIMPSON

There is no portion of a golf course which requires more care at the time of construction, and more attention later in the upkeep, than the area upon which most approaches to the hole will land. What decisive and subtle influences may be made to work upon the ball at just this point!

ROBERT HUNTER

The only thing which should be allowed to interfere with the greenkeeper is the weather.

TOM SIMPSON AND H.N. WETHERED

When one goes to the trouble of placing a bunker across the left side of the green in order to force the tee shot toward the right side of the fairway, why destroy its effect by soaking the green so that any sort of pitch over the bunker will hold?

BOBBY JONES

The best golfing grasses vary in color. They may be red, brown, blue, dark green, light green, yellow, and at times even white and gray. A golf course that is consisted entirely of one shade of green would be merely ugly. There is great charm and beauty in the varying shades of color on a golf course.

ALISTER MACKENZIE

Bring Back the Rabbits!
By Alister MacKenzie

In early days golf was played on public commons or links land, bordering the sea; land which was invariably of light sandy or gravelly nature, and of little value for agricultural point of view, is frequently the best for golf. Links land consisted of rolling sand-dune country, partially covered with gorse, heather, bent and short rabbitty turf. In days of old, a golf course was usually kept by one greenkeeper, who not infrequently acted as professional as well. The rabbits acted as ground staff, keeping the turf short, crisp and free from weeds.

The duties of the greenkeeper simply consisted in cutting the holes and sweeping the rabbit droppings from the greens. Now alas most of these old seaside courses have been ruined by well-intentioned but injudicious efforts of their green committees to improve on nature. The rabbits have been killed off, alkaline fertilizers, fit only for agriculture, have been used, and the sparse dwarf velvety carpet of turf has disappeared, and is now replaced by plantains, daisies, clovers and luscious agricultural grasses; grasses necessitating an enormous amount of mowing, weeding and upkeep.

The greater the amount these clubs have to spend, the more their courses have deteriorated. Not only has the turf been ruined, but there has been a wanton destruction of many of the natural features. The greens have been flattened out, sand hazards, which created the strategy and interest of the holes, filled up, and in too many cases even the undulations of the fairways have been destroyed. The features of links land which the modern golf course architect attempts to imitate (sometimes with indifferent success), have disappeared, so that these glorious natural courses have only too frequently become as dull and insipid as a second-rate inland course.

> We have been visiting Macrihanish at intervals for over thirty years and each time the links has appreciably deteriorated.

There was a course in the wilds of the west coast of Scotland, among most spectacular sand dunes, named Macrihanish. It was scores of miles from any railway station and the only way to get to it was by steamboat and a long carriage drive. Notwithstanding its inaccessibility, the course was so good and the climate so bracing that it became very popular and attracted an increasing number of men who had reputations as players. Some of these players were Open or Amateur Champions, and the natives, dazzled by their reputations, greedily accepted their advice.

We have been visiting Macrihanish at intervals for over thirty years and each time the links has appreciably deteriorated. When we first went there, the course was kept up by one greenkeeper, it was not mowed, except by the rabbits, or rolled. The greenkeeper's duties simply consisted in cutting the holes and filling up any scrapes the rabbits had made on the fairways and greens. It is a remarkable fact that rabbits rarely scrape well-trodden turf, but confine their attentions to bare places on the outskirts of the course, so that even the depredations of the rabbits involved remarkably little labor.

In those early days the turf on the greens and fairways was superior to any I have seen before or since. There was a complete freedom from weeds, daisies or worm casts. One's ball sat up on the closely-cropped turf in a remarkable manner. Each hole was an adventure, there were no guiding flags and no fixed routes, and one could frequently beat an opponent who had greater length and skill, by superior strategy. The annual subscription to the club was ten shillings (two and a half dollars) and there was no initiation fee.

The course was planned by old Tom Morris. Old Tom was thoroughly steeped in the old traditions and spirit of the game. He was a sportsman in [the] best sense of the term; he had no use for arguments based on strict equity. No professional since his time has ever grasped the real sporting spirit of golf architecture in the way he did.

Commander Stuart told me that when he and old Tom first saw Macrihanish, they stood on yonder hillock and old Tom looked round and in a spirit of deep reverence said:

"Eh' mon' the Almighty had gowf in his e'e when he made this place."

As the years go by, Macrihanish is gradually deteriorating. In the first place the rabbits have been destroyed on the clubhouse side of the burn, so that the beautiful velvety turf has been replaced by rich agricultural grasses, daisies and weeds. Beyond the burn, where there are millions of rabbits, the old character of the turf still remains; but as the club accumulates more funds, they use them to destroy their gorgeous natural features.

Almost without exception the old seaside rabbitty turf has disappeared and been replaced by grasses entirely unsuitable for golf. The turf near the clubhouse is usually worse than that farther away as on most seaside links there still remain a few rabbits on the outskirts of the course.

No1 470 YARDS

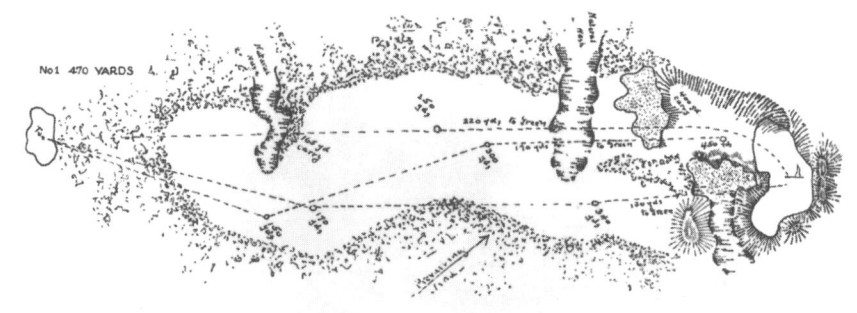

Copyright 1926, by George C. Thomas, Jr.

George Thomas's 1st at Riviera
Thomas believed the strategy of the golf course was the "soul of the game," and built accordingly. The first at Riviera offers options for all players but requires careful planning thanks to the "boomerang" green.

STRATEGY

Writer and artist Charles Ambrose devoted many of his pre-1940 *Golf Illustrated* columns to the emerging art of golf architecture. Fascinated by the mysteriously simple "line of charm," Ambrose was determined to explain to readers why it was reasonable for architects to break up the straightest route to the hole with hazards. Or, the line of charm.

"If Colt made a profession of golf architecture, and Abercromby made an art of it, Tom Simpson has climbed still higher up the ladder that leads to the realm of High Art, if he is not already at the top," Ambrose wrote in 1933.

"To begin with, Simpson is richly endowed with the infinite capacity for taking pains which is said to amount to genius. He picks and chooses his subjects with care, refusing pointblank any commission which may not turn out a success, no matter what inducement may be offered to him to undertake it; but, once he has turned his hand to a job, he sees it through with all his might and main, giving to it the fire of an almost frenzied enthusiast. Frequently words fail him, and he is unable to speak fast enough to describe to you all the beauties of the scene he is about to create. When the flow does come, his language is as picturesque as his imagination.

"He glories in being regarded as the firm friend of the humble rabbit and the sworn foe of the lordly tiger. Time and again does he go out of his way to provide nice little lawns and special stepping stones to help the rabbit to score an easy 5, while the ferocious tiger is made to run hair-raising risks to secure his 4. (Perhaps this is a slight exaggeration of actual fact, but Simpson makes one exaggerate!) He sets out, anyhow, deliberately to frighten the tiger on the teeing ground, while encouraging the rabbit.

"The great secret underlying all Simpson's technical success is clever orientation—by which is meant the angle at which putting green, or fairway, or both are set to the line of play.

"Gone indeed are the days when the great J.H. Taylor was able trenchantly to exclaim, 'What is wrong with the middle of the fairway?' without fear of being gainsaid or doubted by anybody.

"Today, Simpson's crushing reply is, 'Everything! If we are to put up any sort of fight against the modern American expert, to say nothing of the golf ball manufacturer,' he declares, 'we must learn to shoot at an apple and not at a haystack!'"

The spirit of golf is to dare a hazard, and by negotiating it reap a reward, while he who fears or declines the issue of carry, has a longer or harder shot for his second, or his second or third on long holes; yet the player who avoids the unwise effort gains advantage over one who tries for more than in him lies, or fails under the test.

GEORGE C. THOMAS JR.

It is important to emphasize the necessity for the golfer to use his head as much as his hands; or, in other words, to make his mental agility match his physical ability.

TOM SIMPSON AND H.N. WETHERED

The strategy of the golf course is the soul of the game.

GEORGE C. THOMAS JR.

The strategy of golf is the thing which gives the short accurate player a chance with a longer hitter who cannot control his direction or distance.

GEORGE C. THOMAS JR.

When it is more generally realized that a truly fine round of golf represents the accurate fitting together of shots that bear a distinct relation to each other, with the greens opening up to the best advantage after placed drives, then the game will be a truer test of all the mighty ones than so many courses now present.

A.W. TILLINGHAST

A　　　　　　　　　　B　　　　　　　　　　C

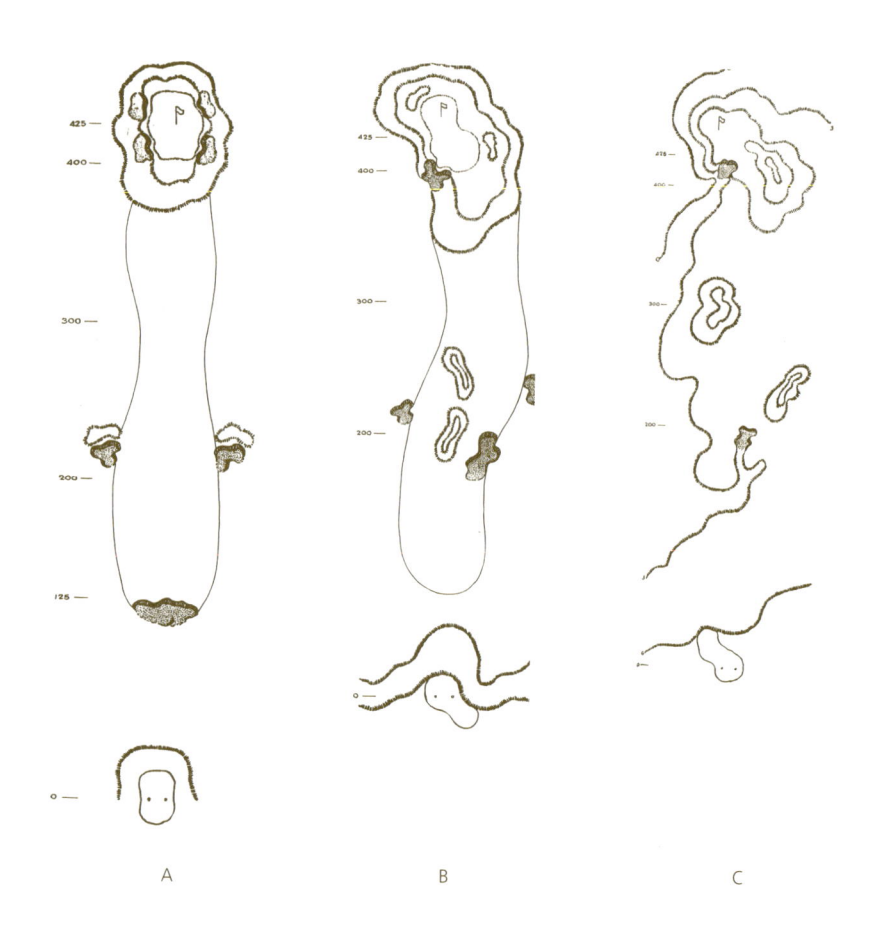

Max Behr's Penal vs. Strategic Renderings

Behr offered the A drawing as an example of a penal hole, and two alternatives with strategy in mind. Of the B drawing, he wrote that it was "a hybrid hole" combining the penal and strategic. The last drawing was an example "wherein hazards are used to create strategy. Not one of them is interested in directly penalizing an error of skill, but their reciprocal relation is such as to compel the golfer to consider whether he can carry the bunker out 200 yards from the tee or slip a blow by it. If he succeeds, his approach to the green is rendered far easier than from any other position he might drive to without taking a risk. It is holes like this that rise to meet the skill of the expert, but which leave the ordinary player to choose his own fate."

The object of golf architecture is to give an intelligent purpose to the striking of a golf ball.

MAX BEHR

... we want our golf courses to make us think. However much we may enjoy whaling the life out of the little white ball, we soon grow tired of playing a golf course that does not give us problems in strategy as well as skill.

BOBBY JONES

Great strategic holes primarily challenge thought. Knowledge of what to do is not immediate. It must be sought. The line of skill is not obvious but is concealed in the line of thought. This first has to be determined, and thought is fallible. Sight is rarely so. On a penal course we see what to avoid. A good shot is the mere evasion of evil. But on a strategic course we must study what to conquer. There are indeed optional safe routes that may be taken. In most cases the ball may be kicked to the hole without encountering a hazard. But *the* shot must weather Hell.

MAX BEHR

Putting the Choice Up to the Player

Architect Herbert Strong joined up with writer George Low to share his thoughts on strategy. Though his name is rarely discussed in modern times, Strong created two of the most important early American designs: Inwood and Engineers. The New York layouts hosted important championships, while opening the eyes of many to architectural possibilities. Strong was the pro at Inwood, which he redesigned in preparation for the 1921 PGA Championship. The outcome was so well received that he went into the design business and created some of the most eccentric designs of the Golden Age, including Saucon Valley's Old Course and Canterbury Golf Club.

With the help of Low, he suggests an interesting design for players of all levels:

"One hears a great deal about the type of golf hole that provides a stiff test for the low-handicap player and at the same time affords the middle class player a run for his 'white alley.' But when it comes right down to locating such a hole and proving it out, that's something different. Such holes are hard to locate because fulfilling the two opposite halves of this contract is pretty close on to an impossibility because it amounts in fact to practically equalizing the games of two types of players, where as a matter of fact six, eight, ten or even more strokes' difference per round exists. It's something like providing an interesting test in the way of a high jump for a jumper who can clear five feet and at the same time leave it interesting for the fellow who cannot clear better than four feet.

"There are, however, ways of fulfilling the two conditions set down above by dividing the problem so to speak, and to the right appears a diagram of a hole, which affords all the interest and thrill of challenge desired both for the low-handicap player and the high-handicap man as well as those of the middle section. This hole offers a divided plan for play. On the left is offered a route for the player who can't get the distance needed to get home on a hole measuring around the 480-yard mark in two shots—and comparatively few can. Yet this route in no sense pampers the player. He will need to hit two fine shots to leave him within easy pitching distance for his third, nor will he have to play short purposely anywhere along the way. Meantime, even though he doesn't get two of his best, he still has a fair target to shoot for on his third, if he is faced, we will say, with a full iron approach.

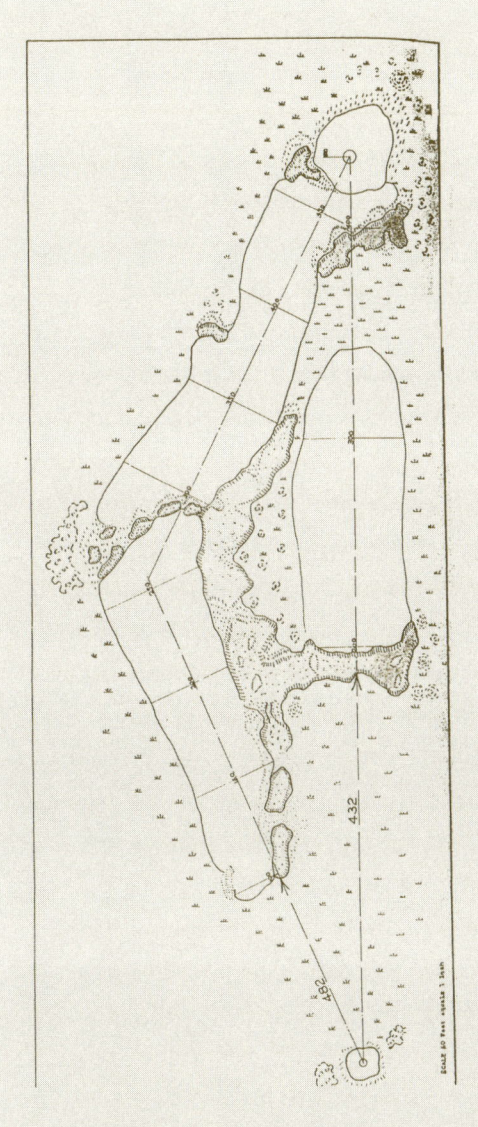

"Now then, look at the alternative offered the heavy slugger. If he chooses to gamble on a carry of two hundred yards, he is given an amply wide fairway to aim at. Assume that his aim is good and that he makes the carry all right. He then has a full shot, either iron or wood, to get home on his second, the distance for the two shots via this line totaling 432 yards as against the 482 of the longer way. But as is the case with his tee shot, the layout is such that this second must be well hit. A topped ball will end up in the rough short of the traps near the green, and if perchance the player does get the ball up, but fails to muster the required distance, he is more than likely to find the traps short of the green.

"Without doubt the trapping on lots of courses detracts from rather than adds to the interest of play. The player who can drive for great distances is entitled to reap his reward for his distance, assuming that he can and does keep the ball straight. And the making of extra-hazardous carries, where he gets his reward, affords one of the finest thrills in the game. On the other hand, the player whose distance is distinctly limited, though he is almost invariably straight, must be given consideration. He too must have something to shoot for, the attainment of which will quicken his pulse, and there is nothing more distasteful to the player of this type than to have to purposely play short of a trap, because he knows that, whereas the long hitters can get over, the best he can show will fail to clear, and leave him trapped for his next.

"The layout picture here meets the foregoing requirements, and puts the issue in each case squarely up to the player. Extra long hitting may prove a handicap, if the player chooses to travel the dogleg route, by leaving the ball on the tee shot in a bunker or the rough, even though the player keeps it straight. If he goes out for great distance and gets it, he is much better off taking the direct route, but he must still reckon with a doubtful avenue of approach to the green, unless he is sure of an approach by the air route practically all the way to the green. Meantime the shorter player has something to shoot for on each of the three shots needed to get him to the green, and probably more of than not, he will be getting his half at least with the sluggers who attempt the shorter but more dangerous route."

… the true line to the hole should not always be the center of the fairway.

TOM SIMPSON AND H.N. WETHERED

I know of nothing so dull as the hole which is played straight away from tee to cup, regardless of how many cross bunkers are put in the way. Such a hole can be made difficult but never interesting, for the playing of it can never involve the least bit of strategy.

BOBBY JONES

The bunkers on the route of the scratch player are evidently not there to punish his bad shots—some of his worst will surely escape them. They are there obviously to call forth the best that is in him. To his weaker brethren they may be the voice of the tempter and the song of the Siren, but to him they are rowels which goad him on to achievements which seem divine. These are the hazards which make golf dramatic. Without them there would be no enduring life in the sport, no vital interest, no delectable thrills—nothing worthwhile to achieve nor anything worthy to be conquered.

ROBERT HUNTER

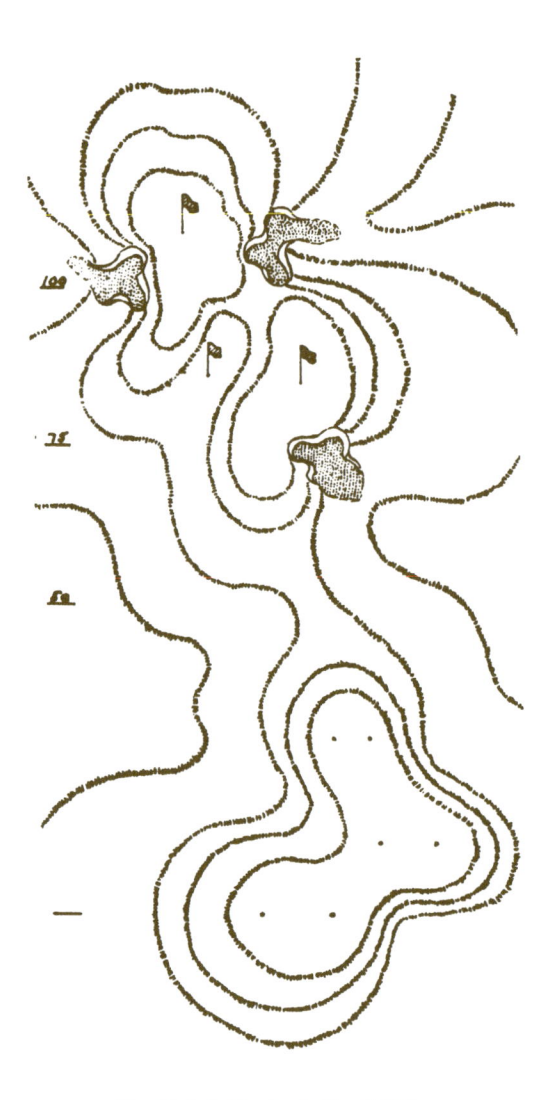

Max Behr's Strategic Short Hole

Behr explained why this par-3 was strategic: "The length of this hole may be varied from 60 to 110 yards. Its character may also be varied by the placing of the pin on the plateau at the back. The player is not required to risk anything. He can use his putter from the tee. But if he wishes to lay the ball dead he must outplay the defensive bunkers. They are not interested in penalizing his ball, but only in defending the hole."

A course that continually offers problems—one with fight in it, if you please—is the one that keeps the player keen for the game.
DONALD ROSS

The true hazard should draw the player towards it, should invite the golfer to come as near as he dare to the fire without burning his fingers. The man who can afford to take risks is the man who should gain the advantage.
JOHN LOW

There is no necessity for artificial barriers. Play does not have to be systematically controlled. An opposite principle is involved. This principle is freedom. And by freedom we compel the golfer to control himself, that is to say, his instincts. If he judges his skill is great enough, he will of his own accord go for a strategic hazard to gain an advantage just as the tennis player will go for the sidelines of the court.
MAX BEHR

■

... a golf course comprises a number of targets, many of them undefined to the eye but more or less deceptively situated, and liable to escape the notice of the superficial observer; and these are to be selected by the player according to his strength or his deliberate choice. The greatest courses invariably offer a choice of alternatives.

TOM SIMPSON AND H.N. WETHERED

■

There are two ways of widening the gap between a good tee shot and a bad one. One is to inflict a severe and immediate punishment upon the bad shot, to place its perpetrator in a bunker or in some other trouble demanding the sacrifice of a stroke in recovering; the other is to reward the good shot by making the second simpler in proportion to the excellence of the drive.

BOBBY JONES

■

There should be two ways to play a hole, one for a physically strong, and one for the man not so strong. The holes should be trapped so that par golf depends upon skill rather than upon physical strength.

DONALD ROSS

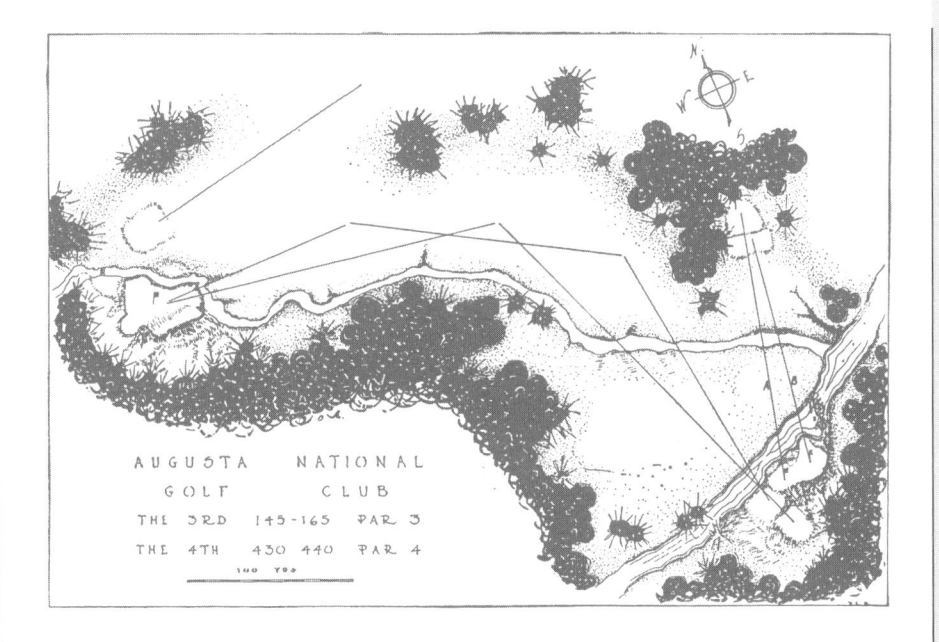

Augusta National's 12th and 13th Holes

With this pre-construction rendering (above), Alister MacKenzie first wrote about the eventual par-3 12th: "The tee is high ground from which the green and stream are very visible. There is a beautiful hill slope beyond the green. 'A' is the medal position for the pin. The green is very narrow at this spot and is wide when played along 'B' route but this involves a long putt across 'A.' It will be noted that stepping stones lead to the green instead of the usual bridge."

For the par-4 13th (then labeled a par-4), MacKenzie wrote "This is a dogleg hole played diagonally over a stream. The straight and courageous player has a great advantage for his first and second shots. It will be noted there is not a single bunker at either of these holes. There are only 22 bunkers on the Augusta National."

MacKenzie and co-architect Bobby Jones later added bunkers behind the 12th green.

The Bulldog Breed Again
Sportsman (in difficulties): "How many are you?"
Opponent: "I'm a foot off the pin in four."
Sportsman: "All right, then; this for a half."

■ HAZARDS ■

No matter how revered they are today, the architects quoted throughout this book constantly were asked to defend their ideas. Hazard placement was often a source of contention. Golfers then, as they do now, objected to man-made hazards—particularly those placed in any place of consequence (usually a location causing the player to hesitate).

Long before this struggle between professional architect and golfer, John Low devoted a chapter of his book *Concerning Golf* to the subject of "unfair" bunkers. His writings would later be consulted by Alister MacKenzie, C.B. Macdonald, H.S. Colt, and other Golden Age figures.

As a member and the best player at Woking Golf Club, Low altered Tom Dunn's design. Low found himself admired and despised for one especially controversial bunker added to the club's fourth hole. Bernard Darwin later wrote that Low's contentious but clever bunker placement so impressed Tom Simpson that it compelled the legendary architect to get into the golf course design profession.

Low recalled one humorous hazard-related story that may sound oddly familiar to anyone who has served on a golf or green committee.

"The other day the Green Committee of a club in which I am interested had the boldness to cut a bunker in the side of one of their putting greens," Low wrote. "When the daring deed was discovered the members assembled round the offending orifice and gazed into it as into a tomb. 'What is this for?' said one, 'it looks like a bunker in the middle of the putting green!' 'Perhaps they are going to relay the turf,' suggested another member. 'It's not so bad just now,' murmured a rather erratic performer, 'but suppose the hole was quite close to the side of that pit, what could one do?' Soon each and all stood silently staring at the yellow sand: a sadder or more hopeless set of men I have seldom seen.

"The bunker was on the seventeenth green, and a vision of the 'last 7,' the seven that takes away all hope and strews the way to the eighteenth tee with small pieces of paper—that vision seemed to be in the eye of each. And yet it seems to me a very reasonable thing to put a bunker in the side of a large putting green.

"If you cut bunkers where no one ever goes, or which can be carried by a child, they cost just as much to make, and no one ever uses them. If you make a bunker beside a hole and the members of a club wish to 'hole out,'—this being an important point in the game—they must go near the bunker, and may sometimes have fun of seeing an opponent working among the sand. Bunkers, if they be good bunkers, and bunkers of strong character, refuse to be disregarded, and insist on asserting themselves; they do not mind being avoided, but they decline to be ignored."

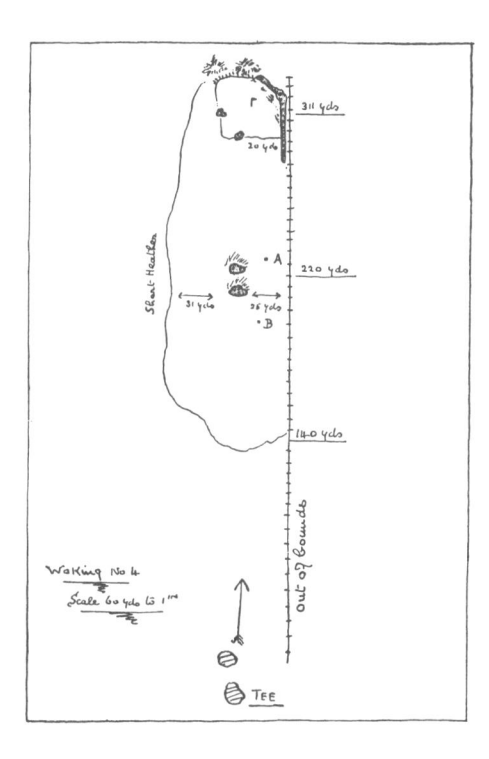

The 4th at Woking
Tom Simpson's sketch of the infamous Woking par-4, a hole redesigned by writer and club member John Low. Simpson wrote, "The carry from the tee on the direct line is 220 yards. The green slopes away from the player and has a sharp tilt left to right, which makes it extremely difficult to stay on if approached from the left, which is the safe line from the tee. The scratch player attempts to reach A with tee shot. The moderate player will get as near B as he can."

The best artificial hazards are usually sand pits so located as to trap badly-hit balls. They are the inanimate fielders of golf, and all golfers strive to follow Keeler's precept of "hitting 'em where the fielders ain't." In brief, the hazards of golf put a premium on the accurate placement of the ball. The mediocre player fears them and cramps his strokes in the effort to avoid them, and his play will not improve until he learns to go at a hazard fearlessly.

A.W. TILLINGHAST

Hazards—how well chosen the name! They are risks; and penalties must come to those who take risks and fail.

ROBERT HUNTER

Just as close as he dare: that's golf, and that's a hazard of immortal importance! For golf at its best should be a contest of risks. The fine player should on his way round the links be just slipping past the bunkers, gaining every yard he can, conquering by the confidence of his own "far and sure" play.

JOHN LOW

The object of a bunker is not only to punish a physical mistake, to punish lack of control, but also to punish pride and egotism.

C.B. MACDONALD

The best looking bunkers are those that are gouged out of faces or slopes, particularly when the slope faces the player. They are very much more effective in that they stand out like sentinels beckoning the player to come on or keep to the right or left.

WILLIAM FLYNN

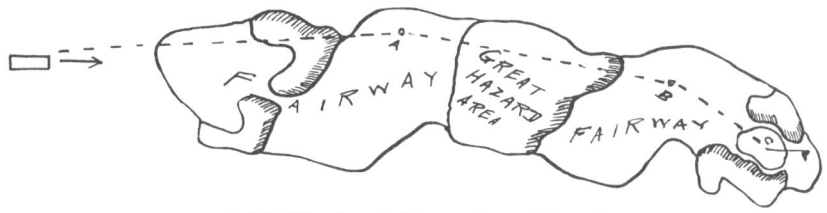

A.W. Tillinghast's "Great Hazard Area"
Tillinghast took partial credit for the idea of Pine Valley's "Hell's Half Acre,"
a mid-hole forced-carry feature that is one of the most famous hazards in golf.
Tillinghast created similar hazards on par-5s at Baltusrol, Baltimore Five
Farms, Bethpage-Black, and Philadephia Cricket Club.

Often, the very highest recommendation of a bunker is when it is criticized. That shows that it is accomplishing the one thing for which it was built: It is making players think.

DONALD ROSS

The stones to the building of architecture are hazards.

MAX BEHR

The risk of going into a bunker is self-imposed, so there is no reason why a player should condemn a bunker as unfair.

C.B. MACDONALD

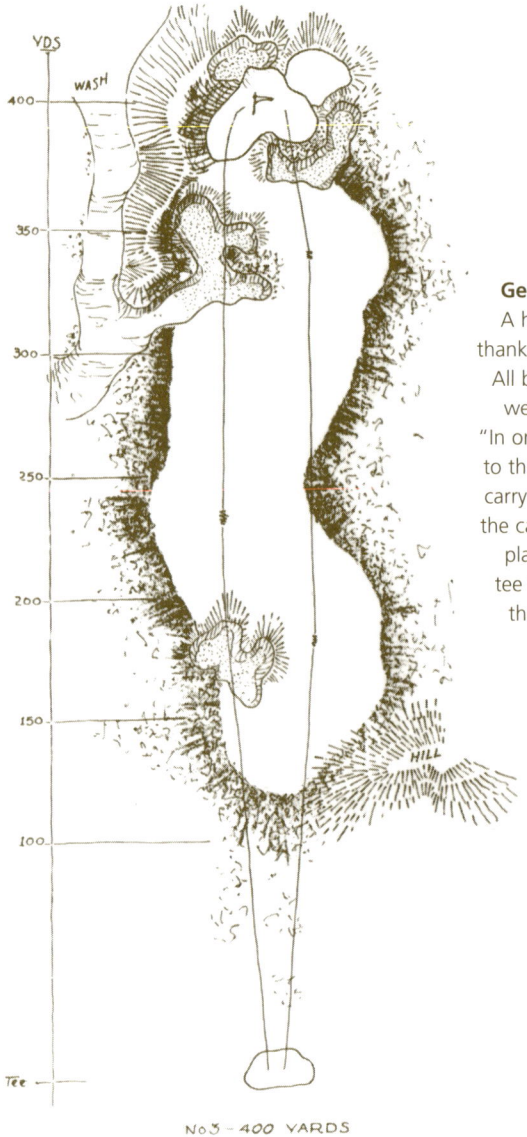

George Thomas's 3rd at Riviera

A hole with classic design strategy thanks to careful placement of hazards. All but the bunker behind the green were constructed. Thomas wrote, "In order to secure the more open shot to the green, it is necessary to make a carry of 180 yards. From the short tee the carry is considerably less. The short player has an open shot from the tee without a carry, but if he avoids the hazard, he has a much more difficult shot to the green."

A hazard placed in the exact position where a player would naturally go is frequently in the most interesting situation, as then a special effort is needed to get over or avoid it.

ALISTER MACKENZIE

Pits which day after day in practice rounds are passed unnoticed, suddenly assume terrible aspects on tournament days, but generally it is the fear of the hazards which in reality is more terrifying than the hazards themselves.

A.W. TILLINGHAST

The great value of a hazard is not that it catches a shot that has been missed but that it forces a miss upon the timid player; its psychological worth is greater than its penal value.

BOBBY JONES

Each stroke comprehends not only an immediate problem but a future problem as well. It follows that every hazard of a hole, even the bunkers that abut upon the green of a three-shot hole, must be felt by the player at the tee. Thus the golfer is forced to assume immediate risks if he wishes to rid himself of future liabilities.

MAX BEHR

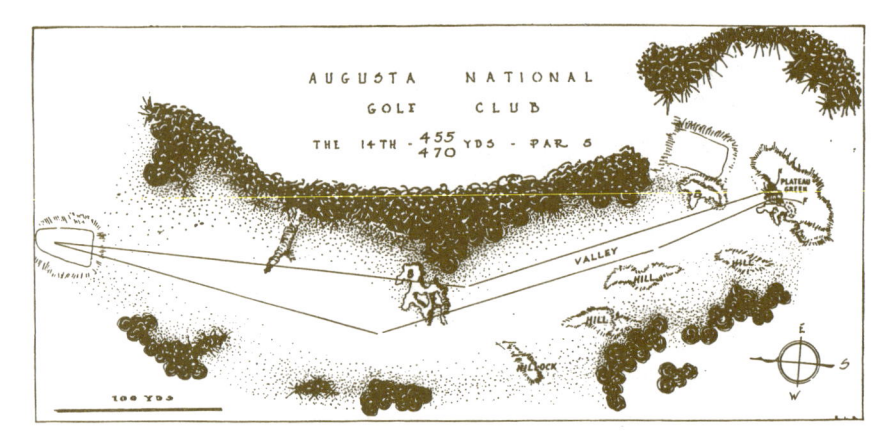

Alister MacKenzie's 5th at Augusta National
Originally the fourteenth and listed as a par-5, the hole became the par-4 fifth when the nines were reversed. MacKenzie wrote, "This is a similar hole to the famous seventeenth road hole at St. Andrews, Scotland. The green is on a plateau and the player who hugs the trees (indicated in black on map) has a visible shot; the player who avoids the woods and steers wide of the bunkers (B) has a blind approach."

All artificial hazards should be made to fit into the ground as if placed there by nature. To accomplish this is a great art. Indeed, when it is really well done, it is—I think it may truly be said—a fine art, worthy of the hand of a gifted sculptor. They should have the appearance of being made with the same carelessness and abandon with which a brook tears down the banks which confine it, or the wind tosses about the sand of the dunes.

ROBERT HUNTER

Charles Blair Macdonald and Hazards

The National Golf Links of America creator was passionate about the subject of hazards.

"When one comes to the quality of the bunkers and other hazards we pass into realm of much dispute and argument," he wrote in *Scotland's Gift—Golf*. "Primarily bunkers should be sand bunkers purely, not composed of gravel, stones or dirt. Whether this or that bunker is well placed, has caused more intensely heated arguments outside of the realms of religion, than has ever been my lot to listen to."

MR. CHARLES B. MACDONALD

He also wrote, "One may rest assured when a controversy between 'cracks' is hotly contested throughout years as to whether this or that hazard is fair or properly placed, that it is the kind of hazard you want and that it has real merit. When there is a unanimous opinion that such and such a hazard is perfect, one usually finds it commonplace. Fortunately, I know of no classic hole that has not its decriers."

Of pot bunkers, Macdonald wrote, "Let the hazard be in the center or to either side or graduated in distance from the hole across the course. A very great number should be pot bunkers, particularly to the side; bunkers in which one can take a full shot with a wooden club are a travesty—some such bunkers as they have at Sunningdale."

Franklin Booth's *View from the 4th Green, National Golf Links*

WATER HAZARDS

If at all possible, the Golden Age architects avoided the construction of artificial water hazards. For some, it was a matter of upbringing. Those who had played early golf, when the cost of a ball was high, never did overcome the frustration of losing balls to artificial creeks, burns, or lakes.

"My Scotch blood comes to the fore again in prejudicing me against any hazards which created the expense, annoyance and irritation of losing balls or even searching for them," wrote the English-born Alister MacKenzie.

"The attitude of golfers and golf committees are amazingly inconsistent regarding water hazards," MacKenzie wrote in another essay. "I have been requested to avoid beautiful lakes and yet on other occasions I have been asked to make a lake at enormous expense when there was not one existing. At other times … I have come across committees whose sole idea consists of putting a dirty little muddy pond somewhere on the course."

It should be noted that the doctor never built "ponds" at Augusta National. His original design incorporated existing creeks and water features. The club converted the creeks into the now infamous ponds guarding the left of the par-4 11th and in front of the three-shot 15th green. Robert Trent Jones redesigned the par-3 16th and added its carry over a lake.

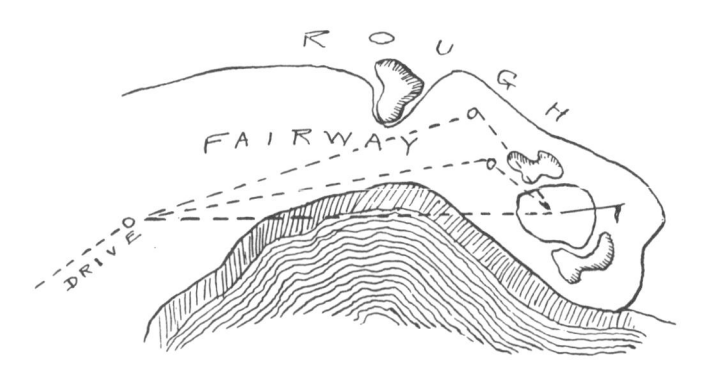

A.W. Tillinghast's "Finely Designed Water Hazard"

As much as he was clearly annoyed by the inclusion of a man-made water feature, MacKenzie delighted in sharing the tale of a Major and his reaction to golf's oldest water hazard.

"Perhaps the most famous of all water hazards is the 'Swilken Burn,' at the first hole on the Old Course at St. Andrews, Scotland," MacKenzie wrote, leading up to one of his favorite stories. "It is gross flattery to call it a burn; in reality it is a muddy sewer, but owing to the peculiar formation of the loop, it makes an ideal first hole.

"In connection not with Swilken Burn but a somewhat similar hazard on another Scottish course that a visitor one day asked what the members thought of the burn as a hazard. He was told that the attitude of a retired army officer summed up the general attitude of the members. 'What is that?' asked the visitor.

"'Well,' was the reply, 'when the Major gets over it, he says to his caddie, "Well ower the bonne wee burn, ma laddie," but when gets into it he says, 'Pick ma ball out of that damned sewer.'"

One natural hazard, however, which is more or less of nuisance is water. Water hazards absolutely prohibit the recovery shot, perhaps the best shot in the game.

WILLIAM FLYNN

Certain it is that the water holes are popular. There is the mental hazard as the great factor, and the average golfer likes to court danger occasionally, provided the architect gives him a safer way around if desired, but probably they meet with so much favor because they generally are attractive to look upon, with a marked individuality.

A.W. TILLINGHAST

There is no thrill in driving over an ugly hazard.

ALISTER MACKENZIE

The difference between a sand trap and water is the difference between a car crash and an airplane crash. You have a chance of recovering from a car crash.

BOBBY JONES

Alister MacKenzie's 12th at Augusta National
MacKenzie's original green sketch for par-3 12th, with Rae's Creek referred to as a "stream." MacKenzie's description has held up: "The bold player will go for the pin on the right, while the less ambitious will steer for the larger landing space on the left side of the green. There is a steep sandy bank covered with beautiful trees beyond the green."

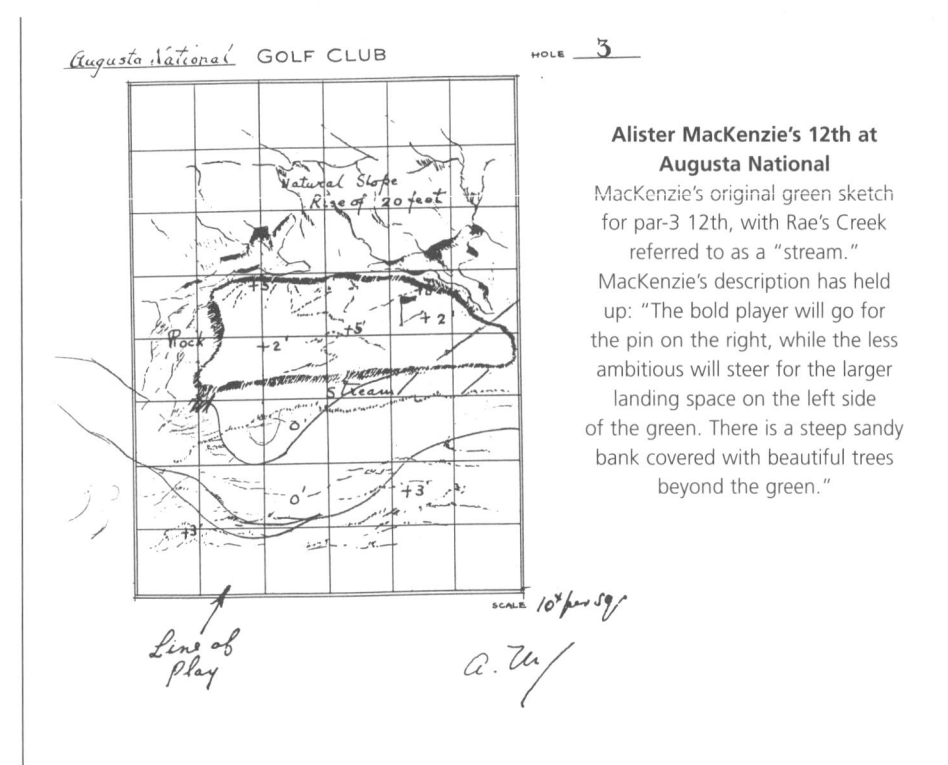

■

There is something so undeniably pleasant about a natural hazard that it seems out of the question to duplicate it artificially. Take, for instance, a creek found on a property. Something about the way banks have shaped themselves adds greatly to their attractiveness. But when a like effect is attempted artificially, it falls far short, no matter what pains and expense are taken. Man cannot do in a few days what nature took years to accomplish.

DONALD ROSS

■

Some players indeed have an antipathy for water which amounts to hydrophobia. But if a clear running stream or a pretty pond with a gravel bed happens to be provided by nature it would be a great pity not to use it.

H.S. COLT

■

I remember many years ago seeing a peppery Major at Stensall in Yorkshire, England, top three balls into an extremely muddy pond. The ugliness of the hazard and his bad play irritated him so much that he threw his club after his ball, then he threw his whole bag in and when his small caddie began to laugh he chucked him in too!

ALISTER MACKENZIE

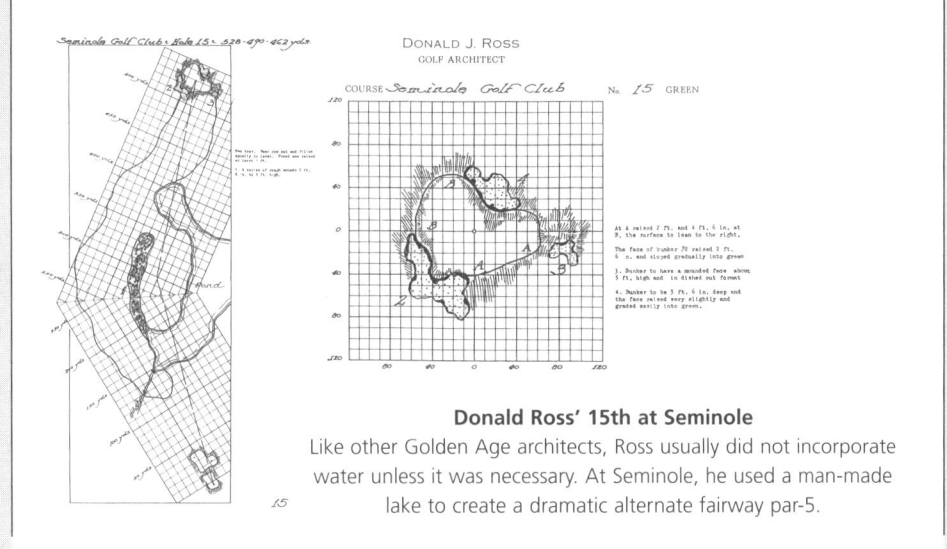

Donald Ross' 15th at Seminole
Like other Golden Age architects, Ross usually did not incorporate water unless it was necessary. At Seminole, he used a man-made lake to create a dramatic alternate fairway par-5.

Franklin Booth's *Punchbowl at the National Golf Links*

■ The GOLFING LANDSCAPE ■

Few of the master architects lived long enough to document their favorite stories either after retirement or when it was safe to offend a client or two. Perhaps some of the architects were too gentlemanly to share those private moments that we'd all love to hear about: the strange and sometimes unbelievable discussions with clients and their friends.

Clifford Roberts cofounded Augusta National with Bobby Jones. Roberts corresponded with Alister MacKenzie on financial and design issues, often complaining that the Doctor wasn't spending enough time on site. MacKenzie was in desperate financial condition and, even after having lowered his fee, found himself forced to point out that the club had not made its contractually obligated design fee payments (nor did it ever pay up).

But long before their spirited exchange of letters ended with MacKenzie's passing in 1934, Roberts shared one of those unique client-architect moments in his autobiography, *The Story of Augusta National*.

"Shortly after I had first met him, I drove the Doc from New York City to a new course in Westchester County named Whippoorwill," Roberts wrote. "Situated on the highest ground in the area, it was extremely hilly. A friend of mine named William Willingham had bought the property just because he admired the place, the splendid scenery, and the numerous deer. Someone suggested that it would be a nice location for a golf course, and Willie, as we called him, had a course built and a club formed. I was invited to join and did so, partly because I was impressed with the exceptional views and one hole in particular that cost $100,000 to construct because part of it had to be cut through solid granite.

"Several members were on hand to greet the doctor and, after he had looked around for an hour or two, they pressed him at lunchtime for his opinion. He responded by saying, 'It's most remarkable,' and that was all they could get from him. On our way back to the city I asked what he meant by the answer he gave my friends.

"'I meant,' said the Doc, 'that it's most remarkable that anyone could be damn fool enough to try to build a course on ground that is so obviously unsuitable for golf.'

"I had taken MacKenzie to see Whippoorwill expecting him to admire it. Needless to say, I felt considerably deflated, especially since it suddenly dawned on me after hearing his brief summation that the doctor was completely right."

■

I have not the slightest hesitation in saying that beauty means a great deal on a golf course; even the man who emphatically states that he does not care a hang for beauty is subconsciously influenced by his surroundings. A beautiful hole appeals not only to the short but also to the long handicap player, and there are few first-rate holes which are not at the same time, either in the grandeur of their undulations and hazards, or the character of their surroundings, things of beauty in themselves.

ALISTER MACKENZIE

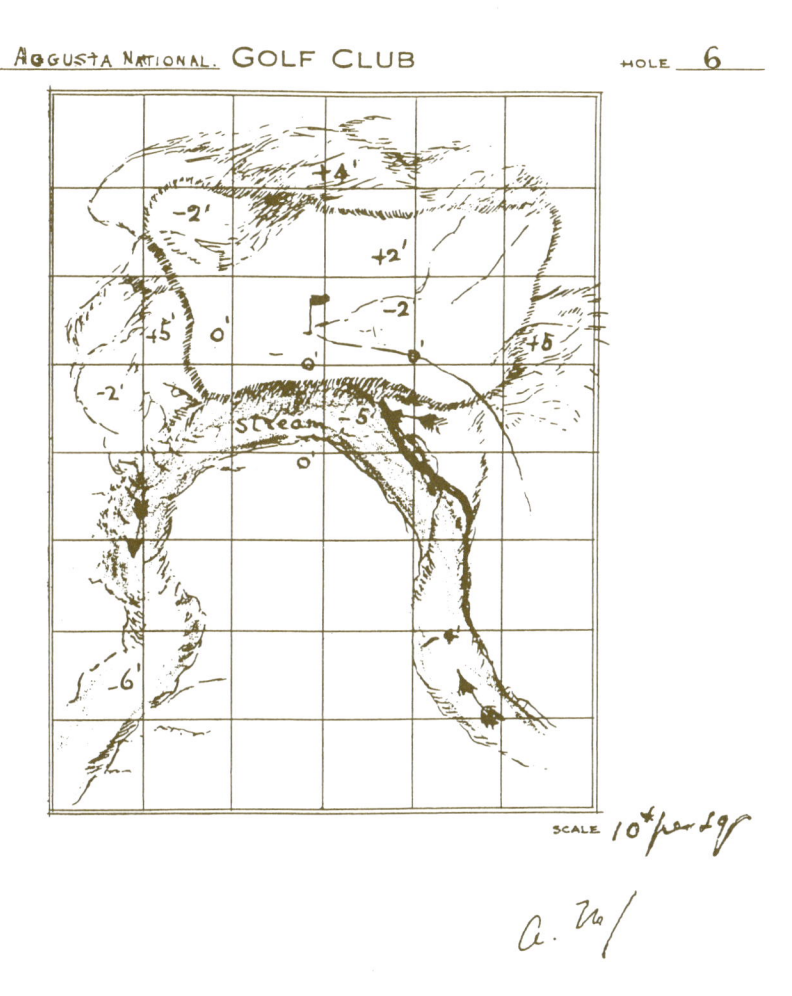

MacKenzie Drawing of the 15th at Augusta National

Alister MacKenzie's original green sketch for the par-5 15th. He wrote, "This is a three-shot hole to most golfers. It is not only an interesting three-shot hole, as one will be maneuvering for position from the tee shot onwards, but also a magnificent two-shot hole, as a skillful and courageous player will, aided by a large hillock to the right, be able to pull his second shot around to the green. A pond in front of the green provides the penalty for the long player who fails to make a perfect second shot."

More than three blind holes are a defect and they should be at the end of a fine long shot only. Excessive climbing is a detriment. Mountain climbing is a sport in itself and has no place on a golf course. Trees in the course are a serious defect, and even when in close proximity prove a detriment. Out of bounds should be avoided if possible. Cops are an abomination. Glaring artificiality of any kind detracts from the fascination of the game.

C.B. MACDONALD

No reason exists why a golf course should not decorate the landscape rather than disfigure it.

TOM SIMPSON AND H.N. WETHERED

When playing golf you want to be alone with Nature.

C.B. MACDONALD

... you can have some large spaces between holes, on which you can plant trees. You thus get the feeling of being in wild and open country, instead of in a small back garden, and your fairways need not resemble a number of parallel and rather narrow streets.

C.H. ALISON

When we build golf courses we are remodeling the face of nature, and it should be remembered that the greatest and fairest things are done by nature and the lesser by art, as Plato truly said.

ROBERT HUNTER

Nearly all good golf holes have some undulation in the surface of the ground that gives them the interest and character that makes them what they are.

DEVEREUX EMMET

… no matter how skillfully one may lay out the holes and diversify them, nevertheless one must get the thrill of nature. She must be big in moldings for us to secure the complete exhilaration and joy of golf. The made course cannot compete with the natural one.

GEORGE C. THOMAS JR.

Nature will often provide us with a small feature which will work in successfully with the scheme for a good hole.

H.S. COLT

How the dear old inland home course looks after a month on the seaside links

The approach to the first hole. (N.B.—A half-topped pull, with a "hair-pin" slice to finish with, is really the shot.)

TREES

What did the Golden Age architects have against trees?

After reading the forthcoming lines of charm, you'd guess they had fallen out of tree houses in their youth, only to grow up determined to rid the world of our tall woody friends.

Explanations for their contempt vary, but the master architects did not hate trees as much as their comments may imply. Instead, they were simply thinking of links golf when building on inland sites. There was also the increasing desire to narrow courses, and architects then or now tend to ask for a wide tree clearance, knowing they still won't get the space necessary to create enjoyable golf.

A.W. Tillinghast may have written most fondly of trees and defended their place on the course.

Except for one tree.

"More than twenty years ago, Mr. Chandler Egan won the championship of the United States at Baltusrol," Tillinghast recalled in 1931. "I played him in the first round of that tournament and at the end of the eleventh enjoyed a lead of one hole. After our drives to the twelfth it looked for a brief moment as though my lead might go to two for my call rested in the fairway within a short pitch to the green, while Mr. Egan had unleashed an unholy hook into a real jungle.

"How he ever got a club to that ball, or what manner of club it was, matters not, but that ball came out plenty. It would have continued its mad flight for a lot more than the player had hoped had it not come in violent contact with a lone tree, which grew immediately by the side of the green for no good purpose.

"After sampling nearly every branch of that tree for a good place to alight, the ball finally decided on a nice spot on the green itself very close to the cup. The birdie 3 evened the match which had looked like two down a moment before. In memory that tree was coupled with one of life's darkest moments. Some years later, I had been retained by Baltusrol to remodel the course and extend it to its present 36 holes. One day the late Mr. Louis Keller, then of the Green Committee, heard the sound of axes eating into a half dead tree and hurried over to investigate. Nearby he found their golf architect looking on and smiling contentedly as he stood on the old twelfth green."

Trees are a fluky and obnoxious hazard.
H.S. COLT

Trees and shrubbery beautify the course, and natural growth should never be cut down if it is possible to save it; but he who insists on preserving a tree where it spoils a shot should have nothing to say about golf course construction.
GEORGE C. THOMAS JR.

TREES

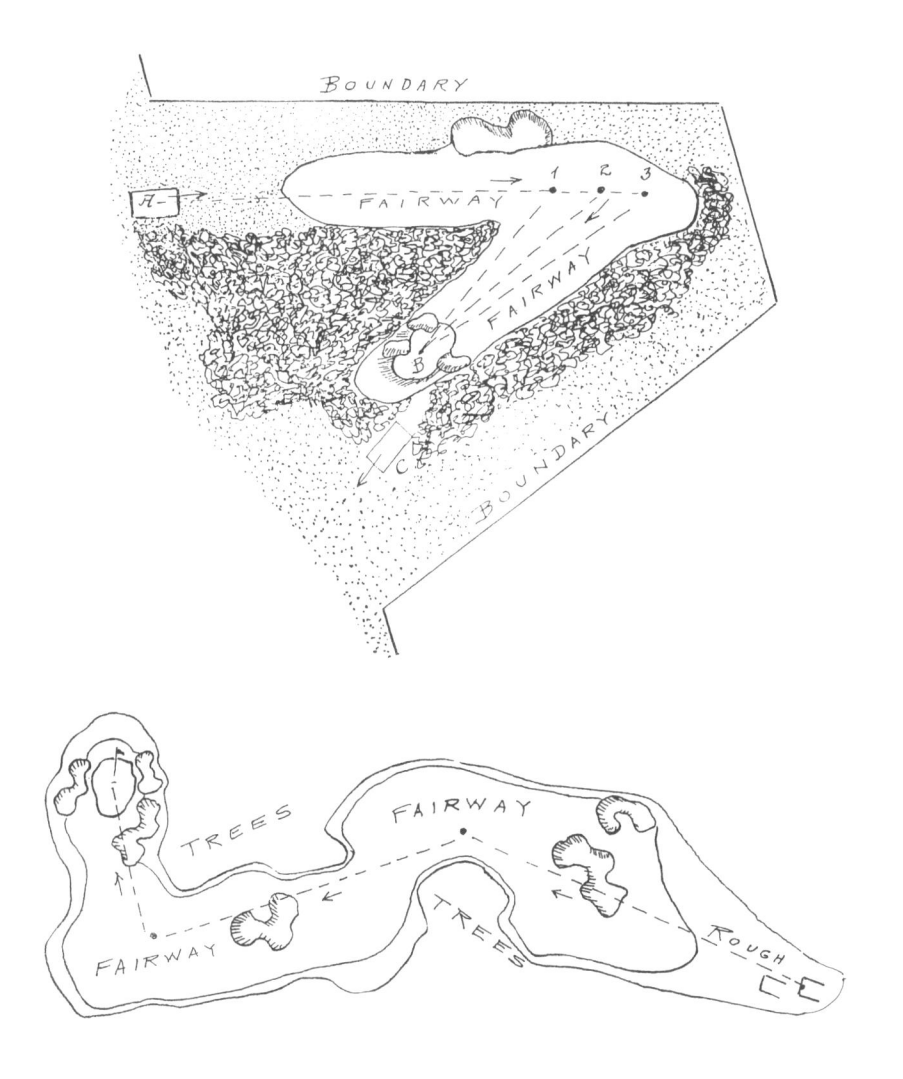

A.W. Tillinghast's "Playing Through Trees"
Tillinghast was not afraid to advocate the construction of golf courses
through wooded sites, though he did give new meaning to "dogleg" with
his near 180-degree hole and the double-dogleg featured above.

***Clearings* by Charles Ambrose**
Artist and writer Ambrose offered these two views in 1933, one with trees and thick underbrush, the other depicting a more joyful golf experience to play through where "clearings" had taken place.

Ambrose wrote, "It is curious how crazy many otherwise perfectly sane people seem to be about trees. To cut down any tree, anywhere, in any circumstances, is an unforgivable sin, even when the felled tree was smothering some other, far finer, specimen behind it. 'Who is Man, to destroy what God has planted?'— that is the usual burden of the objectors' refrain; and the unfortunate official in charge of a golf course has to put up with it."

Often it is possible, by clearing away undesirable and unnecessary trees in the margin of fairways, to open up a view of some attractive picture.

STANLEY THOMPSON

I sometimes take my very life in my hands when I suggest that a certain tree happens to be spoiling a pretty good golf hole.

A.W. TILLINGHAST

Playing down fairways bordered by straight lines of trees is not only unartistic but makes tedious and uninteresting golf. Many green committees ruin one's handiwork by planting trees like rows of soldiers along the borders of the fairways. Alternatively, groups of trees, planted irregularly, create most fascinating golf, and give players many opportunities of showing their skill and judgment in slicing, pulling round, or attempting to loft over them. Some of the most spectacular shots I have ever seen have been around, over or through narrow gaps in trees.

ALISTER MACKENZIE

… as fond as you and I are of them, we still must not lose sight of the fact that there is a limited place for them in golf.

DONALD ROSS

A. W. Tillinghast On Colt's Parallel Fairways

Long before liability insurance and the obsession with planting trees to create "separation" on Golden Age courses, the architects were already battling with committees over parallel holes. Inspired by St. Andrews, the masters saw nothing wrong with such a configuration, as long as the holes were properly designed.

Tillinghast wrote about the issue in 1917:

"In laying out the early American courses, holes frequently paralleled and seldom was any provision made to close off the greens from strokes played on adjoining fairways. As a rule a rather meager strip of rough divided the fairways and as a result the balls which were a bit off line found this rough, but an atrociously bad shot came to rest in a neighboring fairway, where from an inviting lie, the green could be reached without great difficulty. Erring strokes found the rough, but villainous ones were not punished.

"When the golf architect is provided with anywhere from 125 to 150 acres there is but little excuse for the paralleling of holes. Certainly it is

> "When the golf architect is provided with anywhere from 125 to 150 acres there is but little excuse for the paralleling of holes.

more difficult to avoid the evil if the shape of the tract be nearly square and such a bit of land taxes the architect's ingenuity.

"To be sure the deadly straight parallels may be avoided by dog-legging and twisting the fairways, and to punish very wayward strokes the greens usually are heavily bunkered on the same side as extends the adjacent fairway, from which wild and unpunished strokes might be played.

"When H.S. Colt, the English golf architect, was in America several years ago, he made plans for the Indian Hill course at Winnetka, Illinois, and his treatment of the fifteenth and sixteenth holes, which paralleled, is excellent and worthy of study. It may occur to many that he has been rather prodigal in his demands for sand, but in sections where this material is difficult to secure, grass hazards will serve the same purpose."

Franklin Booth's *Redan* at
the National Golf Links of America

■ The REDAN ■

"'Said the North Berwick caddie to Mr. Macdonald when he was on the quest for ideal holes for the coming National Golf Links: 'Here's the hole that makes a man think.'"

At least that's how Macdonald's son-in-law H.J. Whigham recalled the day Macdonald discovered the most reproduced hole in the history of golf course design. The thinking man's par-3: North Berwick-West's Redan.

Somehow, photos of the stern-looking Macdonald make it hard to imagine a scenario where he smiled at his North Berwick caddie and thanked him for such a succinct bit of wisdom. The Macdonald we've come to know through images and his writings probably gave the young looper a strange look and went on to play the hole, perhaps realizing only after playing it that his caddie was on to something.

Here was a par-3 that made the golfer think.

So few one-shotters offer options, but the accidentally designed 15th at North Berwick presents the golfer with many possibilities. In the years since it was discovered, the Redan has been reproduced hundreds of times by architects around the world, most notably in versions by Macdonald and his sidekick, Seth Raynor.

Designers like A.W. Tillinghast and George Thomas reinterpreted the Redan to create their own unique par-3 reproductions. Devereux Emmet went a step further and used the Redan to inspire a par-5 green at his Huntington Country Club design.

Initial impressions of North Berwick's 192-yard, par-3 15th are anything but positive. The mounds and rolls left behind after the sea receded give the West Links their natural contours. The original Redan green complex was placed on a diagonal sloping plateau with cavernous bunkers cut into the facing slope guarding the left and right shoulders of the green.

Serving Officer John White-Melville was credited with naming the hole after his return from a mid-eighteenth-century battle. Melville described North Berwick's difficult par-3 as reminiscent of a formidable fortress he had encountered at Sebastopol. In 1855, the French and British were fighting Russians on the Black Sea's Crimean Peninsula, where the British captured a Russian-held fort. Or in local dialect, a redan.

"Redan" is now part of the English language, defined by the Oxford Dictionary as a "fort" that has "two faces forming a salient towards the enemy."

Even the U.S. Civil War's Battle of Vicksburg featured two Confederate Redan fortifications long before the great golf architects began searching for them amidst the American landscape.

■

You cannot go wrong with a Redan hole.
DEVEREUX EMMET

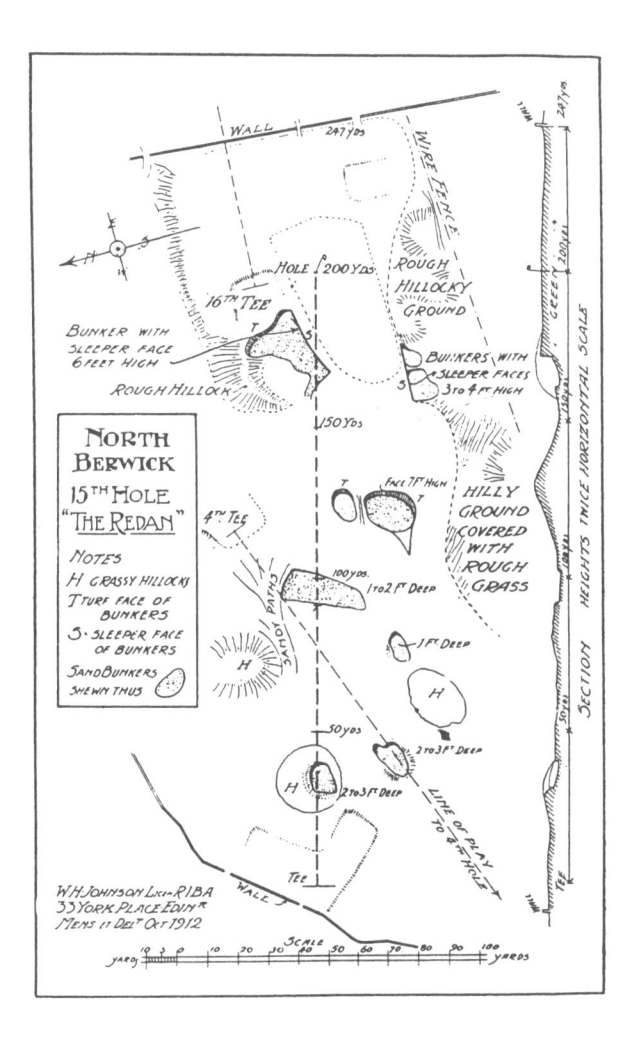

Redan Survey

A look at the original "Redan," North Berwick's 15th. Writer Bernard Darwin characterized the hole in his typical succinct manner: "The Redan is a beautiful one-shot hole on the top of a plateau, with a bunker short of the green to the left and another further on to the right, and we must vary our mode of attack according to the wind, playing a shot to come in from the right or making a direct frontal attack."

Take a narrow tableland, tilt it a little from right to left, dig a deep bunker on the front side, approach it diagonally, and you have the Redan. At North Berwick, of course, all these things were done in the beginning by nature. The only original thing that the greenkeeper did was to place the tee so that the shot had to be played cornerwise, so to speak, instead of directly down the tableland.

C.B. MACDONALD

Those who are acquainted with North Berwick will recognize the influence of the Redan ...Yet it may be said that the Redan, although a world-famous hole, is not a great one. The visibility is poor; the slope on the right which swings into the green is invisible from the tee and there are a number of superfluous bunkers.

TOM SIMPSON AND H.N. WETHERED

Don't let famous holes like those or many others, such as the Alps of Prestwick and Redan of North Berwick, lead you into attempting to reproduce them. In trying to make your course fit certain famous hole treatments, you are certain to be doomed to disappointment. Make your holes fit your course. No other way can be satisfactory.

DONALD ROSS

The golfer playing for his four at the Redan feels certain that he will get it, but the one who plays for a three may easily take a five. In such places the greater burdens are laid on the shoulders best fitted to bear them, and when the hazards are so situated as to accomplish that result, what more can be desired?

ROBERT HUNTER

Max Behr's Redan
Behr depicted a Redan and wrote that it was "a perfect golf hole." He believed so because "it affords the golfer the opportunity of disciplining himself and leaves him free from all penalty if he chooses to play the safe way."

The Redan Hole

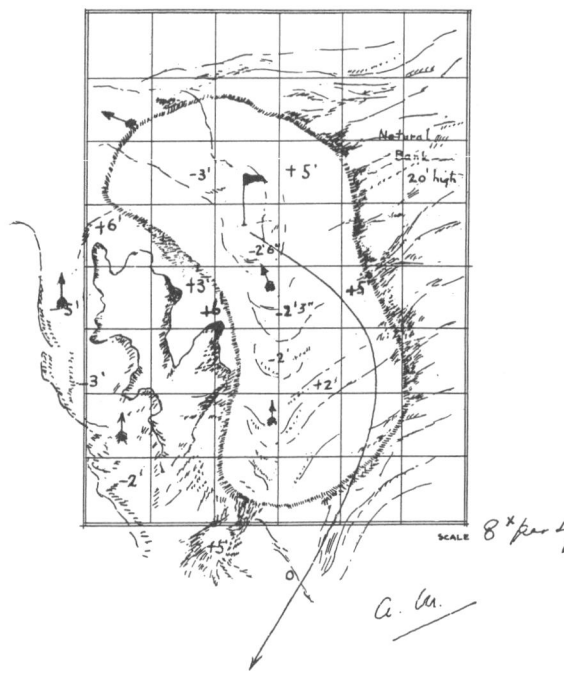

MacKenzie's 10th at Augusta and the Line of Charm

For years golfers have heard about Perry Maxwell's 1937 alteration to the famous downhill 10th at Augusta National, creating the long par-4 we know today. But Alister MacKenzie's green sketch reveals that his original was quite interesting. The strategy was simple: play down the right side to a plateau and open up the best view of the green. Turn the corner and roll down into what is today considered the prime landing area; there, the player would be faced with a difficult and blind approach to a green tucked behind the enormous cape-and-bay bunker that still defines the hole today.

The hole MacKenzie and Bobby Jones envisioned also did not follow traditional design: play to the outside of the dogleg for the best angle of approach. This helps explain why MacKenzie defended Max Behr's case for breaking up the "line of charm" or "line of instinct."

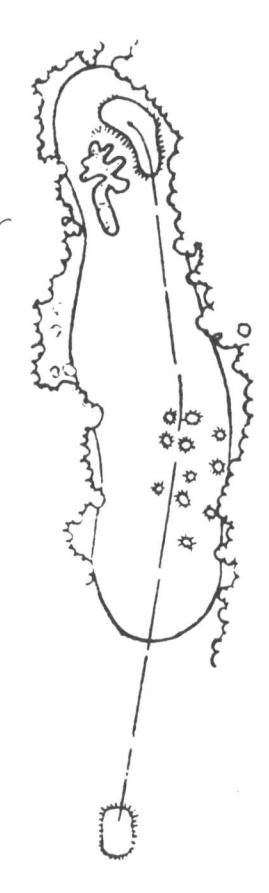

APPROACHES and GREENS

No other architect or player took up the cause of firm approaches and greens like Bobby Jones did. He saw how soft putting surfaces took a beautifully angled or protected green complex and stripped it of its integrity. Jones despised such a trend long before he codesigned Augusta National with Alister MacKenzie, where an emphasis on firm greens was essential to the course's strategic character.

"There can be little question that the great mass of golfers in this country prefer their greens very soft," Jones wrote in the mid-1920s. "Such a condition makes the play much easier for all classes of players, and is in great measure responsible for the fact that tournament scoring is uniformly lower over here than on seaside links in the British Isles.

"There is a close relationship between our two great American preferences, the one for placing our green-bunkering very close to the putting surfaces, and the other for soggy greens which will hold any kind of a pitch, whether struck with backspin or not. The close guarding in many instances makes a soft green necessary if the hole is to be playable, and the easy pitching, on the other hand, makes it necessary to decrease the size of the target in order to supply any test.

"I quarrel with both ends of the proposition, whichever is to blame. These together are the two reasons, I think, why our golf courses, in the main, lack the subtlety of the British links, and why our golf does not demand the strategy or the intelligent planning it should. In my opinion, a properly designed hole should impose a test upon each shot that the player has to make. There should always be a definite advantage to be gained from an accurate and intelligent placing of the tee shot, or a reward offered for a long, well-directed carry over some obstacle. This advantage or reward can only be in the shape of an easier and more open road for the second shot. And when we soak the green with water, we absolutely nullify the advantage which the design of the hole has held out.

"Our expert players are in the habit of playing long iron and spoon and brassie shots bang up to the hole. As long as they can do this, no architect can expect them to worry much about placing the tee shots.

"It seems to me that the ideal green would be sufficiently soft only to hold a properly played pitch—and by 'hold' I do not mean to stay within a very few feet. To carry out the intention of the designer, conditions ought to be such that a definite penalty should be sustained by the player who has played himself out of position."

Green complex design was another frequent topic for the master architects. Most times their imaginative creations amaze golfers, and sometimes those brilliant concepts arose from primitive means. C.B. Macdonald relayed one suggestion from Horace Hutchinson before creating the National Golf Links of America:

"I listened attentively to everything he suggested—where the bunkers should be placed, where the undulations should be created on the putting-greens, etc, etc. I know he impressed on me that the human mind could not devise undulations superior to those of nature, saying

APPROACHES AND GREENS

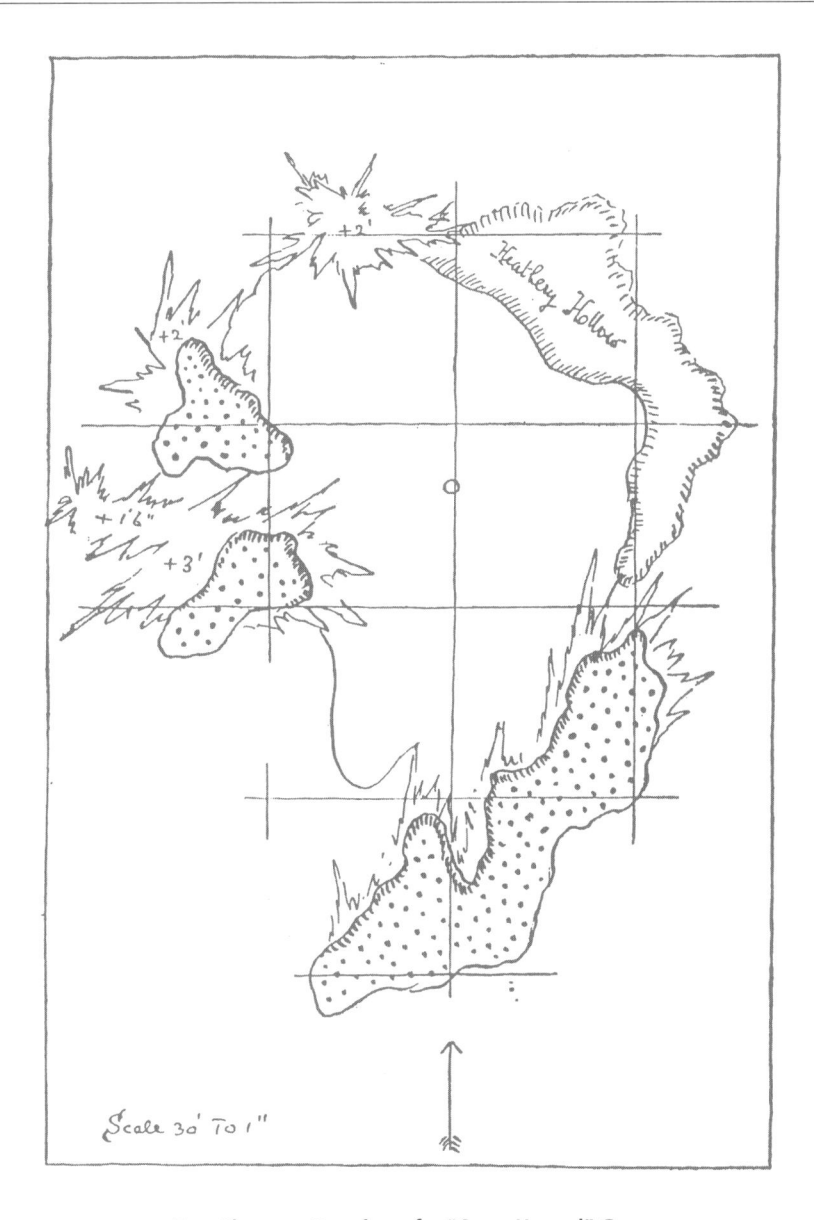

Tom Simpson Drawing of a "Cross-Hazard" Green

that if I wished to make undulations on the greens to take a number of pebbles in my hand and drop them on a miniature space representing a putting-green on a small scale, releasing them, and as they dropped on the diagram place the undulations according to their fall. This I did for some of the National greens where I had no copies of the original undulations which nature had made on the great greens of the world."

■

In this country, we delight to pitch, pitch, pitch, because it is easier than executing a delicate run-up or pitch-and-run.

BOBBY JONES

■

… a vast amount of interest is added to the approach play by the lie of the land in front of these greens. If the player has gauged his shot correctly and struck the ball truly he enjoys the intense pleasure of seeing it run firmly up to the hole; while if his stroke is untruly struck he experiences the almost painful thrill of seeing it shouldered away from the green and perhaps sucked into an adjacent bunker.

C.H. ALISON

■

If driving appeals to the boy, scientific approach play appeals to the man.

H.S. COLT

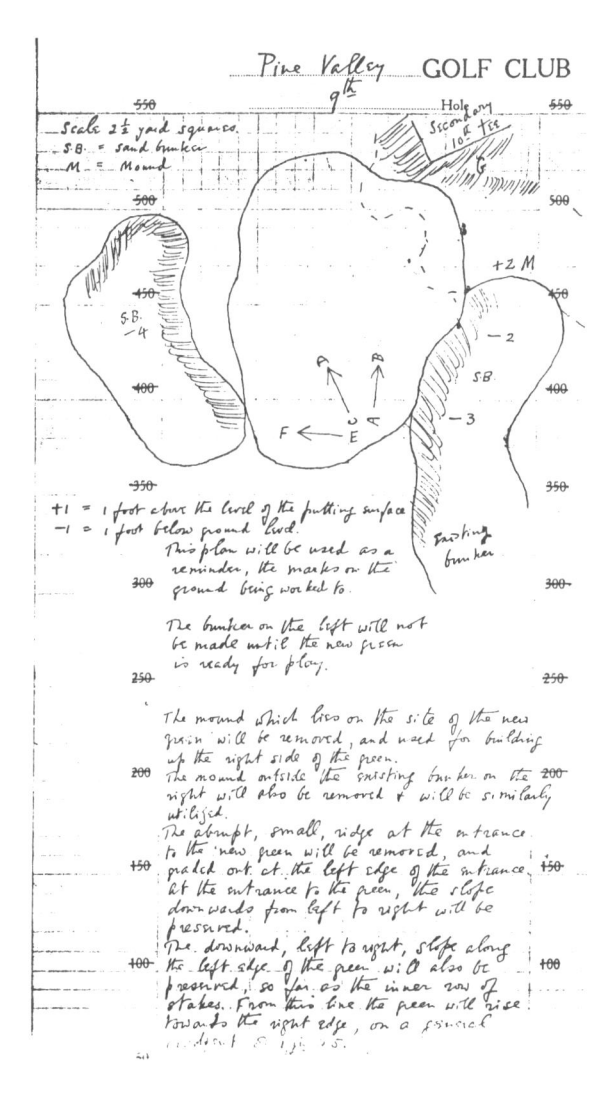

C.H. Alison's Plan for No. 9 at Pine Valley

Around 1920, architect C.H. Alison was asked to analyze George Crump's Pine Valley design. The longtime partner of H.S. Colt, who consulted for Crump on the original design, Alison praised the design but did suggest enhancements to several greens. This is his plan for changes to the par-4 ninth green.

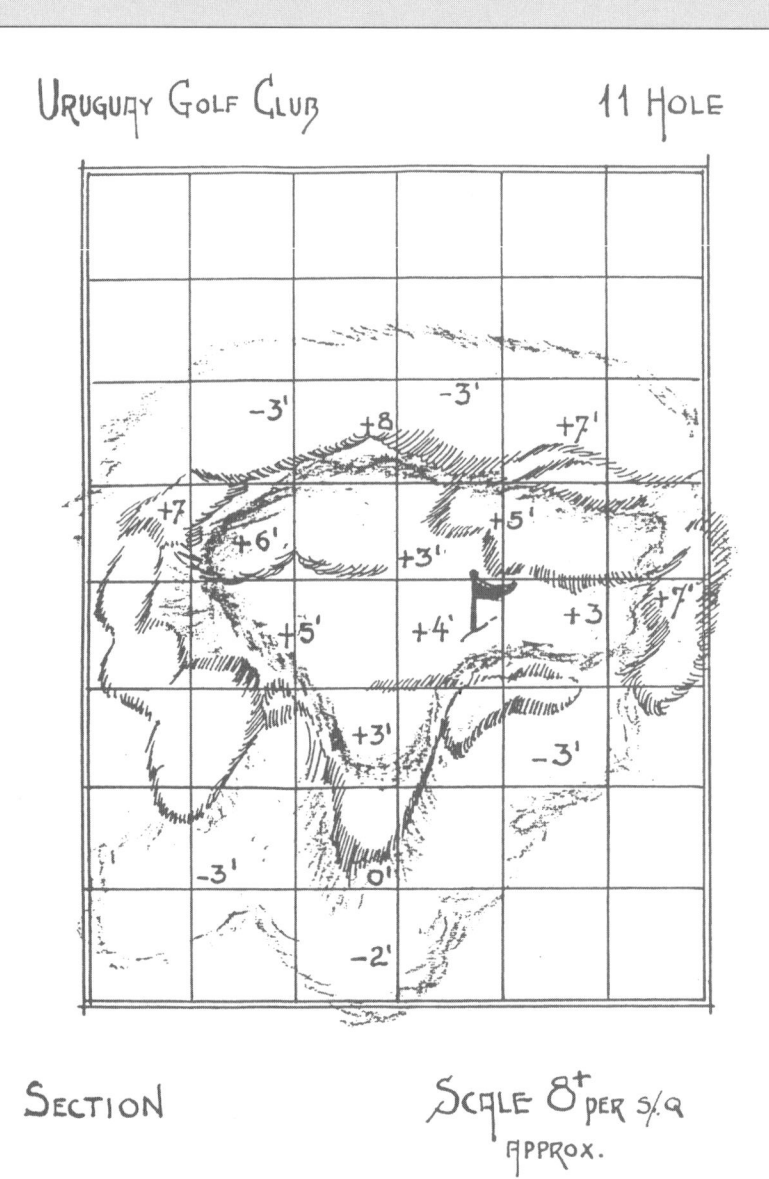

Alister MacKenzie Sketch of Uruguay Golf Club Green

■

Naturalness in a course also implies holes guarded by natural hazards, and more particularly by natural turns and twists in the ground designed by the hand of Providence to tease the cut-and-died approaches.

HORACE HUTCHINSON

■

Every putting green should have a distinctive note, and the ground in front should be carefully studied.

TOM SIMPSON

■

Certain degrees of luck, it is true, can reasonably be judged criminal—as, to take one example, when a fold in the ground is so sharp and boldly pronounced that a matter of inches will determine a very wide deflection in the direction a ball will take to the one side or the other. At St. Andrews the slopes are never abrupt to this degree, but invariably so shallow that frequently either side of a slope can be made use of in order to get near the pin.

TOM SIMPSON AND H.N. WETHERED

■

Putting greens to a golf course are what the face is to a portrait.

C.B. MACDONALD

Golf Course Architecture

**Courses Designed
Construction Supervised...
Personal Examinations** *and Reports*
Original Conceptions *of* **Greens Modeled**

A·W·TILLINGHAST·Inc

HARRINGTON · PARK · N·J · · · TELEPHONE · CLOSTER · 1435

A putting green has features just like a human, or, at least, it should have to be worthy of the name. Of course, there are many which are no more impressive than the vacant, cow-like expression of some people, but then again, there are some with rugged profiles which loom head and shoulders above the common herd, and the moment we clap eyes on one of these, impulsively we murmur, "Ah! There's a green for you!"

A.W. TILLINGHAST

Putting greens constructed with relation to the length and topography of the hole are the making of a real golf course.

DONALD ROSS

It has often been said that architects have designs for 18 greens and that the same ones are used over and over again on the various layouts. A successful architect of today does not follow that system. His greens are born on the ground and made to fit each particular hole.

WILLIAM FLYNN

Tillinghast's List of Evils in Golf Course Design

10. Holes laid out backwards.
9. Climbs to higher levels too suddenly and not gradually enough to make play not arduous.
8. Holes playing along slopes rather than into them.
7. Holes playing directly into hill slopes.
6. Changing a hole because a certain class player did not like it.
5. Greens too freakish for any shot.
4. Greens too small for long shots.
3. Greens too large for small shots.
2. Greens that drain too much.
1. Greens that don't drain.

Franklin Booth's *Alps at the National Golf Links of America*

BLINDNESS

Bobby Jones enjoyed dealing with adventurous, even unpredictable holes. But there was a learning curve involved before Jones reached this Zen-like attitude toward quirky architecture, exemplified by his notorious tirade at St. Andrews in 1921. Like many, the then twenty-year-old Jones hated the bizarre holes and blind shots. But soon thereafter, Jones began to understand the elements that turned every round into a fun adventure.

Jones learned to savor design features that asked him to merge his imagination and craftsmanship, knowing that it would separate better players from their many fine competitors. Local knowledge, blind shots, and changing conditions rewarded intelligence as much as they would help the shotmaker.

Blindness was and continues to be the most complicated design trait, one that Jones embraced at a time when it was considered "unfair" by an emerging union of golf professionals.

"A friend of mine, who has recently returned from a visit to St. Andrews, tells a story," Jones wrote in his syndicated newspaper column.

"Upon starting his round, he had been provided with one of the picturesque old Scotch caddies who are so much a part of the place. My friend said that he happened to be playing particularly well this day and his caddie was exhibiting an avid interest in his game. (He *must* have been playing well.) On each tee he would be told exactly where to drive, and on the way to his ball he would be instructed on the placing of the second shot to obtain the most favorable position for the approach.

"This had gone on for some time when my friend hit one tee shot better than the rest, which delighted the old caddie's heart. It was a good long one, and the old fellow had declared that it was exactly on the proper line. They walked on down the fairway, with the caddie explaining all the while about the playing of the next shot and praising my friend's excellent drive. Finally, they topped a sizable knoll, and there, nestling serenely in a small bunker about the size of a wash tub, was my friend's ball. The old caddie was abject.

"'Well, I been a-carrying clubs here for thirty-seven years and I never saw that bunker before.'

"That is the adventure of St. Andrews. Every hazard is not out in the open, where it can plainly be seen, and there are no lines of rough down either side of the fairway marking the area in which the tee shot must land. You size up your problem and you pick your own way to solve it. But you are likely to learn something surprising each time you play a hole. It is not a course one would like particularly well at first, because the unseen hazards and rolls are likely to be considered unfair. But, as Dr. MacKenzie contends, the adventure holds interest."

■

On two-shot holes it is highly desirable in many cases to compel the player to place his tee shot so that his shot to the green may be clear, and if not properly placed, the shot to the green may to some extent be blind.

DONALD ROSS

Blindness is the one type of hazard in golf which contains the element of mystery. If we were not all so concerned with our scores, and, instead played golf for the pleasure in playing the strokes, blindness would not be so abhorrent to us as it is today.

MAX BEHR

More than three blind holes are a defect and they should be at the end of a fine long shot only.

C.B. MACDONALD

There may be a certain amount of pleasurable excitement in running up to the top of a hillock in the hope of seeing your ball near the flag, but this is a kind of thing of which one gets rather tired as one grows older.

ALISTER MACKENZIE

No hole may be condemned as blind if it is so because the feeble hitting of the player makes it so. Some of the best holes are great because visibility of the green is only gained because a fine shot opens it to sight.

A.W. TILLINGHAST

No More Lost Balls! The Patent Vacuum Ball Finder

SLIPPING INTO the ROUGH

Max Behr despised the emerging concept of rough. In 1926, he referred to the "hay fields" at the U.S. Open hosted by Scioto. Behr saw rough as an added feature introduced solely to thwart driving distances that had begun to overwhelm otherwise fine architecture.

Behr had a strong amateur record and was one of the game's most respected voices during the Golden Age's later years. His most notable playing accomplishment was a loss to Jerome Travers in the finals of the 1908 U.S. Amateur. Behr started and edited *Golf Illustrated* from 1914 to 1918, then moved West to write about his interest in golf architecture while designing several fine courses, including Lakeside Golf Club in Hollywood, Rancho Santa Fe in San Diego, and Montecito Country Club. He also consulted on several redesigns, including that of the Olympic Club's Lakeside course.

Hollywood's Lakeside has changed since Behr's day, but in 1931 Bobby Jones filmed many of his short films for Warner Brothers there and also played most of his recreational rounds at the links-like course. Behr's anti-rough philosophy surely rubbed off on Jones and Alister MacKenzie, who would soon build Augusta National on many of the principles Behr was advocating in magazine articles.

To the Golden Age architects, rough did not exist on their pallet of design ploys.

Behr was the first to protest the emergence of "rough," a tacked-on feature that has since become a standard component of modern design and a prime element of the penal-school approach. To the Golden Age architects, rough did not exist on their pallet of design ploys.

"Each stroke comprehends not only an immediate problem but a future problem as well," Behr wrote in 1927. "It follows that every hazard of a hole, even the bunkers that abut upon the green of a three-shot hole, must be felt by the player at the tee. Thus the golfer ... is forced to assume immediate risks if he wishes to rid himself of future liabilities.

"The confinement of width of play by the rough precludes to a great extent the creating of future threats," Behr wrote. "And even where they exist, the player whose ball has found the rough has not a lie to make a direct attack upon them. He must content himself with a negative shot. Therefore the penal idea that makes a virtue of rough with its penal bunkers, robs nature, the opponent, of deploying herself strategically. And that simply means intelligently.

"The golf architect, therefore, is not at all concerned with chastising faulty strokes. It is his business to arrange the field of play so as to stimulate interest. And interest 'implies concern, not with ourselves, but with something real independently of us.' And that is exactly what a penal bunker is not. It is a reality that stands in relation to us; something provided for our special benefit. It does not exist to protect the hole, something real independent of us and with which we are most concerned to play our ball into, but exists merely as a mirror of our faults.

"Thus the penal school puts the cart before the horse. And the golfer instead of pitting his skill against an intelligent opposition of hazards, is driven to a battle with himself. This means an absolute negation of interest. And the reason why most golfers stand for it is simply because they still are at that stage where their principal concern is in hitting the ball. They are learning to walk, and pat themselves on the back when their balls do not slip into the gutter of the rough."

Rough grass is of no value for protecting danger points; it has no effect in keeping people straight, but merely prolongs the length of time players are in the danger zone.

ALISTER MACKENZIE

The lost ball feature of rough is an ever-present evil.

GEORGE C. THOMAS JR.

■

... owing to the stress today placed upon competition in golf, golf architecture has come to be rationalized. The old road which seemed to wander with no intent or purpose, and from which wandered off byroads to fool the traveler, has now become a well-posted concrete highway. Every inducement is offered to step upon the accelerator as long as one can keep the car of skill from slipping into the rough.

MAX BEHR

■

Long grass entails too much searching for balls.

C.B. MACDONALD

■

Narrow fairways bordered by long grass make bad golfers. They do so by destroying the harmony and continuity of the game and in causing a stilted and a cramped style, destroying all freedom of play.

ALISTER MACKENZIE

■

Instead of a golf course providing an adventure of the spirit because of its demand for an intelligent, courageous application of skill, they will be reduced to mere trap shooting galleries, and the card and pencil will become the final arbiter of the golfer's excellence.

MAX BEHR

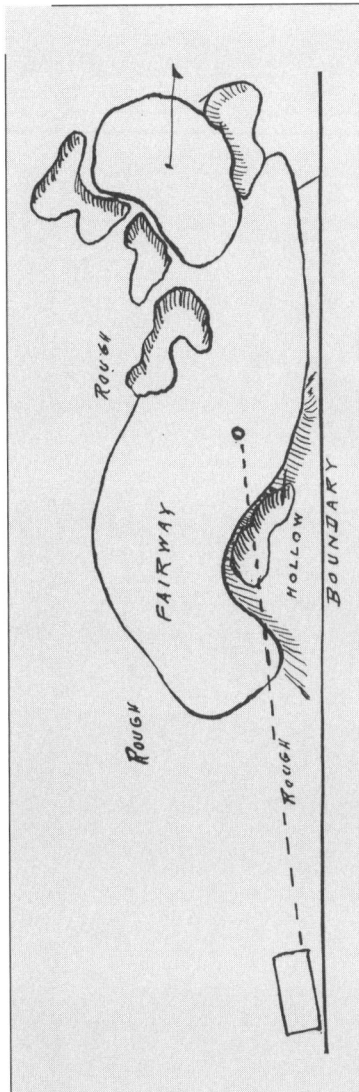

Tillinghast, Boundary Holes, and Rough

A.W. Tillinghast was one of the few Golden Age architects to refer to "rough." Tall grass guarding the sides of a hole has become an integral part of design, a trend the master architects anticipated with little enthusiasm.

In this drawing, Tillinghast pencils in where rough would belong and also depicts a "boundary hole," which he wrote in 1918 was "never desirable."

He continued, "When it is necessary to hug a boundary, an effort to make that boundary help the hole should be made. It is a mental hazard, and every player really fears a boundary quite as much as any hazard on the course. So if he is courageous enough to place his shot close along the danger line there should be an adequate reward for the effort. The sketch illustrates the point far better than any words of mine. It shows the advantage gained by placing the drive over on the right-hand side of the fairway in the direction of the boundary. From this point the second shot to the green is comparatively easy. Danger has been courted and a reward for the brave effort is provided. The sketch also illustrates how a hole may be swung slightly away from the boundary rather than absolutely parallel with it."

Member (in background): "What's the matter with
our worthy secretary to-day?"
The Other: "Oh, he's terribly upset. It's a competition
day, and he hasn't had a single complaint about the course
or the lunch, or the drinks, or the cigars. He feels sure
there must be something wrong."

COMMITTEES, PLAYERS, and CRITICISM

Charles Blair Macdonald might not have fared well in today's "it's all good" world where everyone is entitled to their opinion, no matter how uninformed those views may be.

Macdonald was not a man who cared to hear just any old opinion. He paid his dues, did his homework, and figured things out on his own (at least when it came to golf). History has proven that he was a man of unique vision.

This never stopped golfers from offering suggestions. So to remind folks how little he enjoyed hearing their odd design theories, Macdonald had a solution. When a member made a suggestion for the National Golf Links, C.B. might take the idea if it was a good one. Then he'd send them a bill for making the modification.

The Canadian-born and Chicago-bred Macdonald also saw the American "obsession" with equity endangering golf. Fairness would not only ruin the potential for interesting architecture, but, Macdonald believed, it would lead to misguided, uninformed committees or noted players criticizing design based on personal misfortune.

"So many people preach equity in golf. Nothing is so foreign to the truth," Macdonald wrote in a "rambling thought" near the end of his memoir, *Scotland's Gift—Golf*. "Does any human being receive what he conceives as equity in his life? He has got to take the bitter with the sweet, and as he forges through all the intricacies and inequalities which life presents, he proves his mettle. In golf the cardinal rules are arbitrary and not founded on eternal justice. Equity has nothing to do with the game itself. If founded on eternal justice the game would be deadly dull to watch or play. The essence of the game is inequality, as it is in humanity.

"The conditions which are meted out to the players, such as inequality of the ground, cannot be governed by a green committee with the flying divots of the players or their footprints in the bunkers. Take your medicine where you find it and don't cry. Remember that the other fellow has got to meet exactly the same inequalities. Johnny Low says it is this idea of equity with which the brains of so many golfers are obsessed, and at the bottom of all it is the outcry against the stymie.

"I do not like to refer to people who are always trying to tinker with the rules of the game. They are to me heretics. One group of men make an effort to increase the size of the hole; another group think putting too important and desire to call a stroke on the putting green one-half stroke. God forbid!

"If you have a good sporting game, for heaven's sake don't try to improve it. Your business is not to improve the game *but to improve your play*.

"The scoring habit of American golfers is a pernicious habit, much to be deplored, and if persisted in will result in the destruction of the eternal conception of the game in its highest sense."

COMMITTEES, PLAYERS, AND CRITICISM

Secretary: You'll find the course has been altered
a lot since you were here.
Strenous Friend: Really! I'm afraid you'll find
it has been altered more when I go.

What Our Poor Secretaries Have to Put Up With
It: "That new bunker at the 8th is positively monstrous; why, if you slice at all badly from the 6th, you are in it!"

Does the average player really know what he likes himself? When he plays it successfully, it is everything that is good, and when he is unsuccessful it is everything that is bad.

ALISTER MACKENZIE

A man may be a very good golfer and yet know little about golf architects and golf architecture.

CHARLES BANKS

It is my belief that too many American courses are retarded in proper development and improvement by unintelligent although doubtless well-intended criticism and advice from the locker rooms. Without a doubt, there exist more amateur course architects and turf authorities among the members of some of our clubs than there are following these crafts professionally.

A.W. TILLINGHAST

How often do we hear players criticize a bunker that is placed for a carry as being an unfair one if they cannot carry it?

DONALD ROSS

No real lover of golf with artistic understanding would undertake to measure the quality or fascination of a golf hole by a yard-stick, any more than a critic of poetry would attempt to measure the supreme sentiment expressed in a poem by the same method. One can understand the meter, but one cannot measure the soul expressed. It is absolutely inconceivable.

C.B. MACDONALD

One learns by bitter experience how difficult it is to escape hostile criticism when one makes a hole of the adventurous type.

ALISTER MACKENZIE

In speaking of courses, each man believes that his own is far and away better than most others. He may admit his greens are poor, or that the trap on No. 6 is badly placed, or what not, but nevertheless, he insists that outside of such minor things, his golf home is superior to most. He brings to mind the niblick shot he played in such and such a match; where else could that have been done? He saw Hagen take a 78 on his course, and no one can prove to him that they have a better layout at so and so. It is remarkable how this holds good.

GEORGE C. THOMAS JR.

COMMITTEES, PLAYERS, AND CRITICISM

Being particularly anxious that we should have one perfect hole on our new course, we canvassed separately the opinions of six of our leading links architects as to the construction. Their ideas we adopted in toto, and feel that now we have at least one ideal hole! P.S.—450 yards round the corner is the green where the real difficulties concentrate.

■

Every golfer is inclined to have very decided views upon the merits of a course or the merits of a hole. Sometimes it may be that his exceptional abilities for playing a particular stroke assist him materially in forming his opinion, and possibly—although no doubt one may be wrong in this suggestion—his want of skill urges him to decide with no uncertainty that a particular hole is not golf at all, and that a particular bunker is the creation of a madman or of an ill-natured idiot.

H.S. COLT

■

How often have we known committees, presumably consisting of men of intelligence, receiving the statement that golf is played for fun, with eyes and mouths wide open in astonishment? It is always difficult to persuade them that the chief consideration that should influence us in making any alterations to a golf course is to give the greatest pleasure to the greatest number. Any change to a course that does not do this is manifestly a failure.

ALISTER MACKENZIE

■

Millions and millions of dollars have been spent on golf courses, and millions more in changing them. Most of these mistakes have been made by club committees assisted by golf professionals.

DEVEREUX EMMET

■

I do not suggest for one moment that people are not entitled to express their opinions as to what they like or dislike, but when they go to the length of saying that some particular feature is good or bad, they are more often than not influenced by some peculiarity of their own play.

TOM SIMPSON

■

No man learns to design a golf course simply by playing golf, no matter how well.

BOBBY JONES

■

Criticizing a golf course is like going into a man's family. The fond mother trots up her children for admiration. Only a boor would express anything else than high opinion.

C.B. MACDONALD

■

Competitive golf is chiefly responsible for this tendency to design courses on principles of absolute and relentless justice.

TOM SIMPSON AND H.N. WETHERED

A New Method of Standardisation of Golf Balls
Every ball hit with more than a two-hundred yards impact, immediately explodes. Penalty, one stroke and cost of new ball.

The BALL PROBLEM

Bernard Darwin first broached the ball subject in 1923, only to declare fifteen years later that, "the architects have done nobly; they have fought the good fight, but it ought not to be a fight. The fact that it threatens to become so is the fault of the ball."

However, prior to the late 1920s and early '30s, previous changes in the ball had been well received by architects.

"There have been two great changes in the ball," wrote C.B. Macdonald in *Scotland's Gift—Golf*. "First, the introduction of the gutta-percha ball, replacing the feather-stuffed ball about 1850; and second, the Haskell or rubber-cored ball of half a century later. Each change improved the driving power of the clubs, increased the number of players enormously, and affected many things from courses to rules."

As the ball improved during the 1920s, it became apparent that architecture would struggle to keep up. Most of the Golden Age architects voiced concerns about a knee-jerk reaction to lengthen or alter designs, simply to accommodate the latest "pill." Discussions raged, and many architects appealed for a standardized ball. By 1927, even Bobby Jones was in favor of a reduced-flight tournament ball to keep existing architecture relevant.

In 1923, Darwin debated the improved golf ball's influence on the ground game versus the aerial game.

The Depression and Second World War led many to forget the discussions on this sensitive subject. This might explain how traditions have been ignored to produce today's situation, where it has somehow become the task of architecture, as Max Behr put it, to lock up "this wild desire for distance just as we cage wild animals."

In 1923, Darwin debated the improved golf ball's influence on the ground game versus the aerial game.

"The question of the limitation of the golf ball's power seems once more to be coming into the realm of realities," Darwin wrote. "I had grown accustomed to regard it as a dwelling in a land of dreams and shadows.

"How difficult a question was brought home to me a few days since when listening to an argument about it between some friends of mine, good golfers every one. Said two of these strong men and mighty hitters before the Lord: 'The ball must always be played in the air. To get it there and keep it there is the crown of skill.' To them answered another, not a great hitter but a canny and cunning player with a long head and one who knows the game withal. 'That seems to me,' he said, 'a very arbitrary statement. For my part, I think that the game of golf should be played along the ground.'

"I fancy he made his assertion a little more dogmatic than he would have otherwise done, because the other side had adopted so high-handed an attitude, but still in the main he meant what he said. To him the crown of skill was in keeping the ball down, in making the ground subservient to his purpose. So there we were at a complete impasse.

"For myself, though I thought it wiser to say nothing, I held a third view, namely that the ideal golfer is he who can get the ball up when he wants to and keep it down when he wants to and that the conditions of the game should be such as to give him scope for doing both.

Perhaps that is the pusillanimous middle view of a trimmer, one who only wants to be at peace with both sides.

"But after all, the real reason for putting some limit to the flight of the ball seems to me to be rather far removed from our discussion. I do not greatly care about helping either the man who hits the ball up or keeps it down. I do want to help the man who objects to walking 7,000 yards in the course of a game of golf.

"At the beginning of the 19th Century, there were on the Links of Leith but five holes and each of the five was between 400 and 500 yards long. Men played then with feather balls. Corresponding holes with the modern ball would be between 600 and 700 yards long. I suppose three rounds of the five holes constituted a match. Just think of fifteen holes all over 600 yards! Doubtless the men of Leith were heroes. Nevertheless I do not desire to relapse into their state of heroic barbarism."

Concerning Long Driving

The constant experience of rearranging bunkers, necessitated by the ever-increasing length to which the modern golf balls can be driven, is causing the greatest dismay to our green architects. We can only see one way out of it. Have the bunkers on wheels. They can be adjusted to the requirements of the latest balls, and with a little sand thrown round the base are ready to use.

All architects will be a lot more comfortable when the powers that be in golf finally solve the ball problem. A great deal of experimentation is now going on and it is to be hoped that before long a solution will be found to control the distance of the elusive pill.

WILLIAM FLYNN

Now that the ball-makers have successfully ruined most of our leading courses, it remains for the golf architects to so design the greens that they shall be both difficult of access and that the putting shall demand care and skill in judging slopes and undulations.

HERBERT FOWLER

Pleasure in obtaining length is only a matter of relativity.
ALISTER MACKENZIE

The deterioration of skill brought about by the present ball has caused a mischievous repercussion throughout the length and breadth of golf. The inordinate distance the ball can now be driven has caused in golf architecture a very definite infirmity of principle as all deductions from quantity values are apt to induce. Quantity must be opposed by quantity. Consequently the size of our greens and the width of our fairways have become restricted, and the rough made damnable.
MAX BEHR

I should never care to argue for anything which would lessen the difficulty of the game, for its difficulty is its greatest charm. But when, in spite of vast improvement in the ball, in seeking to preserve the difficulty and to make scoring as hard as it was in the old days, we make the mistake of destroying the effect of skill and judgment in an important department, I cannot help protesting.
BOBBY JONES

■

Time was, and not so many years ago, when a hole 400 yards long on average ground was a good two-shot hole for the star players; now, the same hole is perhaps a drive and spade for the better-class golfers.

WILLIAM FLYNN

■

One of the difficulties with which we have to contend is that any marked limitation of the flight of the ball is certain to be unpopular for some time after its inauguration. Golfers would dislike to find that they were unable to carry a bunker they were formerly able to do. They would feel as though they had suddenly grown old. Something very drastic ought to have been done years and years ago. Golf courses are becoming too long.

ALISTER MACKENZIE

■

The question before the golfers of the world is plain as a pike-staff. Are they going to be sportsmen and accept a ball that requires skill to propel, or, in their infantile worship of mere distance, are they going to continue to be downright game-hogs?

MAX BEHR

The "Improvement" in Golf Balls—What It Is Coming To
Golfer: "Confound it, that's the third consecutive time you've outdriven me by 100 yards. I can't make it out. I hit mine well enough!"
Opponent: "Perhaps you are playing with a yesterday's ball!"

DONALD J. ROSS

makes a specialty of laying out golf courses on modern lines, and of re-arranging existing ones.

He is justly regarded as being pre-eminent in this line.

DONALD J. ROSS,
1108 Northampton St.
HOLYOKE, MASS.

MODERN GOLF ARCHITECTURE

RECONSTRUCTION AND HAZARD CREATION

WRITE FOR ILLUSTRATED BOOKLET

A·W·TILLINGHAST

25 W·45 ST·   NEW YORK CITY
              and
           MUTUAL LIFE BUILDING
                PHILADELPHIA

GOLF COURSE ARCHITECT
Design and Construction
William B. Langford
621 N. Central Ave.
AUSTIN STATION — CHICAGO

COLT & ALISON

GOLF COURSE ARCHITECTS
EXPERTS IN LANDSCAPE WORK

LONDON	PARIS
7 Montpelier Terrace, Knightsbridge, S.W.	8 Rue Léon Bonnat (16)

AMERICAN BRANCH
Capt. C. H. Alison & L. E. Lavis

NEW YORK	DETROIT
110 East 42nd Street	1217 Penobscot Bldg.

DONALD J. ROSS   **WALTER B. HATCH**, Assistant
Golf Architecture and Construction
Supervision of Maintenance
Pinehurst, N. C., until April 15th
After April 18th, 1032 Beacon St., Newton Centre, Mass.

MACKENZIE & EGAN
Golf Course Architects

OFFICE: AGNEW & BOEKEL
FEDERAL RESERVE BANK BLDG.
SAN FRANCISCO

DR. A. MACKENZIE	ASSOCIATE	H. CHANDLER EGAN
Cypress Point Golf Club, Pebble Beach	F. H. Bickleton, Box 152 Santa Cruz	Pebble Beach or Medford, Oregon

---

CHARLES H. BANKS

GOLF COURSES OF DISTINCTION

Designed and Constructed

Associate of the late Seth J. Raynor

**331 Madison Avenue
New York**
Tel.: Murray Hill 10163

W. HERBERT FOWLER
GOLF ARCHITECT

Among the courses laid out or remodeled by Herbert Fowler in California, 1920-1921, are:—

- The Ambassador Golf Club, Los Angeles; opened July 16, and declared by Charles B. Mayo to be "The finest inland course I have ever seen."
- The Los Angeles Country Club; second eighteen holes.
- The Presidio Golf Club; remodeled course, to be opened this fall.
- The Crystal Springs Country Club; new course.
- Del Monte and Pebble Beach. The old historic Number One course is considered today as fine a test of golf as there is on the Pacific Coast.
- Burlingame Country Club; plans for enlarging and remodeling.
- Sequoyah Country Club; course remodeled.
- Menlo Country Club; plans for remodeling.
- Del Paso Country Club, Sacramento; lengthened and remodeled course.
- Capitola-by-the-Sea; plans for eighteen-hole seaside links.
- The Olympic Club of San Francisco; second eighteen holes seaside links.
- San Francisco's municipal links at Lincoln Park; plans for remodeling.

Mr. Fowler, who is now in England, expects to return to California in October. All communications and inquiries for terms, etc., should be addressed

V. HERBERT FOWLER   Care Pacific Golf and Motor
127 MONTGOMERY ST., SAN FRANCISCO

Dr. ALISTER MACKENZIE
GOLF ARCHITECT

105 W. Monroe St. Chicago	604 Federal Reserve Bank Bldg. San Francisco	331 Madison Ave. New York

APPENDIX

THE ARCHITECTS

C.H. Alison (1882–1952) A fine player and member of the Oxford and Cambridge Golfing Society, Alison joined H.S. Colt's design firm prior to World War I and worked on many noted projects, including Sunningdale, Wentworth, and redesigns at two British Open rotation members, Royal St. George's and Royal Lytham and St. Anne's. Alison is noted for his solo work while on a Far East swing in the early 1930s, creating such world-renowned courses as the Kasumigaseki and Kawana Golf Clubs; in the United States, he planned the once-amazing Timber Point on Long Island and created a master plan for Pine Valley that played a significant role in fine-tuning the New Jersey layout into the top course in the world. With Colt, Alison co-authored *Some Essays on Golf Architecture*, published in 1920.

Charles Banks (1883–1931) A longtime construction assistant to Seth Raynor and Charles Blair Macdonald, Banks worked on several of the duo's finest projects before starting his own practice. Banks met Raynor soon after he graduated from Yale and later helped in the construction of his alma mater's layout. In his solo work, Banks stuck to the trademark Macdonald/Raynor look, replete with squared-off edges to his wildly contoured greens, deep grass-faced bunkering, and holes built to mimic the principal features found on the world's more interesting designs. And, like his mentors, Banks typically included a version of the "Redan" and other renowned holes in his work. Banks layouts of note include Forsgate Country Club (East) and Essex Country Club in New Jersey, Tamarack in New York, and Bermuda's Castle Harbour, near C.B. Macdonald's Mid-Ocean.

Max Behr (1884–1955) A noted golfer who reached the finals of the 1908 U.S. Amateur, Behr attended Yale and played on three national championship teams there. The founder and first editor of *Golf Illustrated*, Behr later took great interest in golf architecture after moving to California in 1918. There, he designed Lakeside in Hollywood and Rancho Santa Fe in San Diego, and consulted on the redesign of the Olympic Club's Lakeside course. Behr wrote frequently on all subjects of golf. He was a renowned rules expert and book collector who published a pamphlet titled "What Is Amateurism?" A member of the Royal and Ancient Golf Club of St. Andrews, Behr wrote numerous articles for American and U.K. publications on golf architecture, but never published a book on the subject.

Harry S. Colt (1869–1951) A Cambridge graduate who practiced law for a number of years, Colt became so fascinated with golf architecture that he dropped his law work and became the first full-time professional architect. His first design was in London during the early 1900s. Colt later added two key associates. First was his lifelong partner in design, C.H. Alison, who handled the firm's work in North America and Japan. There was also a brief partnership with Alister MacKenzie, whom Colt met while working at MacKenzie's home course, Alwoodley, in England. Colt wrote numerous articles on the subject, but most of his finest writings were saved for *Golf Course Architecture*, a short but sweet text written with C.H. Alison. Colt was the first to assist George Crump in building Pine Valley and made important contributions to the world's favorite course. Colt also redesigned and created the modern versions of Sunningdale, Wentworth, and St. George's Hill, three of England's most celebrated inland courses. His redesign of storied Muirfield remains his most famous work in Scotland, while Royal Portrush in Northern Ireland is consistently considered one of the world's best courses.

Devereux Emmet (1861–1934) Even though Emmet served as an advisor to his close friend C.B. Macdonald at various times during the construction of the National Golf Links, he had actually designed a fine course on his own well before Macdonald's masterpiece was constructed. Emmet was a fine player and aristocrat who traveled to Europe annually to survey several of the most famous holes of the British Isles for use in the planning of the National Golf Links. Emmet's Garden City Golf Club remains somewhat similar to the original design, with several important changes having been made by Walter Travis. Emmet designed over 100 courses during his career, including many layouts on private estates, Congressional in Washington, D.C., and Marion Hollins' Women's National Golf Club, a course designed solely for women. He wrote all too infrequently on design.

William Flynn (1890–1945) Flynn emerged while working under Hugh Wilson at Merion before starting his own successful firm. At Merion, Flynn supervised construction of the club's famed East course and, some years later, carried out a renovation for Wilson, whose failing health prevented him from overseeing the work. Following World War I Flynn created a partnership with construction specialist Howard Toomey, and the two went on to create some of America's finest courses, including a massive redesign of Shinnecock Hills in 1930, Cascades in Virginia, Atlantic City G.C. in New Jersey, Philadelphia Country Club in his home state, Cherry Hills in Colorado, and a renovation of The Country Club in Brookline, Massachusetts. Flynn's prophetic collection of writings appeared in the USGA Green Section Bulletin.

Herbert Fowler (1856–1941) Described by Bernard Darwin as one of "the most gifted architects" of his time, Fowler's first design effort may have been his finest, the Old Course at Walton Heath. He spent two years between 1902 and 1904 building the Surrey, England course for friends of his wealthy father who had commissioned Fowler thanks in part to his successful amateur golf career. Walton Heath led to more work in the British Isles, including his redesign work at Royal North Devon and Royal Lytham and St. Anne's. Fowler soon branched out to the United States in a brief partnership with Tom Simpson. Herbert Fowler's most impressive work in the United States remains at Cape Cod's Eastward Ho! Fowler's 1921 redesign of Los Angeles Country Club was supervised by George Thomas, and Fowler is considered responsible for advising Pebble Beach to make its finishing hole a par-5. His best work with Simpson overseas may have been Cruden Bay, their 1926 creation in Scotland. Fowler contributed several essays for books and magazines during his career.

Robert Hunter (1874–1942) Hunter was a well-known social worker, author, and thinker before he entered the golf course design business as an associate of Alister MacKenzie. Hunter and MacKenzie first joined forces and took over the Raynor design commissions at Monterey Peninsula Country Club and the new Morse development, Cypress Point Club. Hunter was also appointed to a committee overseeing the major reconstruction of Pebble Beach Golf Links in time for the 1929 U.S. Amateur. But Hunter devoted most of his time to the Cypress Point project, supervising construction and communicating with architect Alister MacKenzie when the doctor was not present. Hunter also commuted to southern California to supervise work on the Valley Club of Montecito. Soon after the Valley Club's completion and the successful opening of Cypress Point, Hunter and his wife retired to Montecito. Though he contributed to one of the most important designs ever created, Hunter's real legacy is found in his writings. His timeless treatise on design, *The Links*, was published in 1926, and many consider *The Links* and other assorted essays by Hunter to be the finest words written on golf architecture.

Horace Hutchinson (1859–1932) The first golf editor of *Country Life Magazine*, Hutchinson grew up playing the wild and controversial Westward Ho! Another Oxford man, Hutchinson complemented a fine amateur golfing career by writing several classic books and designing several fine early layouts. Hutchinson was the first to comprehensively cover golf course design and was also the first to offer design criticism in print. His *British Golf Links* (1897) remains both an astounding production and a valuable examination of old British Isles golf courses. Other noted Hutchinson books include *Hints on Golf*, *Golf in the Badminton Library*, *Famous Golf Links*, and *The Book of Golf and Golfers*. He also wrote a golf course murder mystery. His first design experience was an 1886 collaboration at Royal Eastbourne. He followed that with Royal West Norfolk in 1892, supervised revisions to Ganton, redesigned Le Touquet in France (writer P.G. Wodehouse's home course), and handled the design of Royal Ashdown Forest.

Bobby Jones (1902–1971) The greatest amateur golfer of all time, Jones retired from serious competitive play in 1930 to devote himself to the creation of Augusta National Golf Club. Codesigned with Alister MacKenzie, the course reflected Jones' love of strategic St. Andrews. Jones wrote about golf architecture in his books and syndicated column, and made a habit of studying courses more thoroughly than perhaps any other great player in the game's history.

John Low (1869–1929) No writer was more widely cited by Golden Age architects than Low and his book *Concerning Golf*. Though not lengthy, Low's chapter on strategy formed the basis for many architectural defenses of bunker placement. Low did not do much designing, but his involvement with Woking Golf Club earned the praise of Bernard Darwin, H.S. Colt, C.H. Alison, Horace Hutchinson, and Tom Simpson. Low twice nearly won the British Amateur and was founder of the Oxford and Cambridge Golfing Society.

Charles Blair Macdonald (1856–1939) Canadian by birth but rooted in Chicago, Macdonald was the first to build and design an 18-hole course, the Chicago Golf Club, in 1893. He became the first great player in American golfing lore, winning the inaugural United States Amateur in 1895. Though remembered for his course designs, Macdonald was a rules authority and one of five founders of the USGA. He spent years conceiving and designing his "ideal course," the National Golf Links of America, before designing several other classic courses with his construction engineer, Seth Raynor: Piping Rock, St. Louis CC, Lido, The Links, Mid-Ocean, The Creek, and Yale. Macdonald's *Scotland's Gift—Golf* is a cornerstone of golf literature.

Alister MacKenzie (1870–1932) Master course designer MacKenzie designed some of the greatest courses in the world: Royal Melbourne in Australia, Augusta National in Georgia, and California's Cypress Point Club. He traveled the world, designing and redesigning over a hundred courses with the help of several noted associates who had successful careers of their own, including Perry Maxwell, Chandler Egan, and Alex Russell. MacKenzie also collaborated with author Robert Hunter and golfing great Bobby Jones. Before becoming a golf architect, MacKenzie worked as a doctor during two wars and briefly in private practice. His writings on the subject are classics: *Golf Architecture* and *The Spirit of St. Andrews*, along with numerous magazine articles published throughout his career.

Perry Maxwell (1879–1952) A successful banker who took up golf at the age of thirty, Maxwell became one of America's most important but least known great architects. His résumé remains impressive, with two Midwestern gems in Southern Hills and Prairie Dunes (9 holes), not to mention major redesign work at Augusta National and Colonial. Some of Maxwell's creative instincts may have been influenced by a brief but successful collaboration with Alister MacKenzie in Michigan, where Maxwell oversaw construction of MacKenzie plans for the University of Michigan Golf Club and the brilliant Crystal Downs.

Willie Park Jr. (1864–1925) The winner of two British Open championships, Park laid out his first course at the age of twenty-two, filling in for his more famous father. The Innerleithen design job launched a career that led to nearly two hundred designs or redesigns in Europe and the United States. Park was the first architect to charge a flat design fee and also one of the first to write about golf architecture, submitting "The Laying Out of a Golf Course" for *The Game of Golf* (1896).

Donald Ross (1872–1948) After a stint as Royal Dornoch's greenkeeper, Ross emigrated to America at the turn of the century and took the job as both pro and greenkeeper at Oakley Country Club in Watertown, Massachusetts. Ross soon converted the rather benign and dull layout into a sporty test of golf, impressing James Tufts and his wealthy family. Ross was then invited to become course designer of the Tufts family resort in Pinehurst, North Carolina. Word spread quickly about Ross's work at Pinehurst, and he became known as an architect worthy of hire. Over the next forty plus years, Ross designed or remodeled over 350 courses, and he continued to refine his beloved Pinehurst No. 2 until his death in 1948. A compilation of his commentaries on architecture was discovered and published in 1996 under the title *Golf Has Never Failed Me*.

Tom Simpson (1877–1964) Simpson studied law, but his artistic sensibilities drove him to golf; he played most of his games at Woking in England while also making a study of course architecture. Though he had started his own law practice, Simpson closed it in 1910 to pursue golf course design with Herbert Fowler. After developing a small portfolio of designs with Fowler, Simpson joined forces with Phillip Mackenzie Ross and famous golfer Molly Gourlay. Simpson was responsible for a great deal of sensitive restoration work to various courses in the British Isles that had deteriorated during the First World War, including modifications or restoration to Ballybunion's Old Course, Muirfield, Sunningdale's New Course, and Royal Lytham and St. Anne's. Simpson was also a brilliant artist and writer. In 1929 he co-authored *The Architectural Side of Golf* with H.N. Wethered. Simpson also wrote many other articles on course design.

George C. Thomas Jr. (1873–1932) Amateur architect and author of the seminal *Golf Architecture in America*, Thomas designed three courses in the eastern United States before moving west to join forces with Billy Bell. Together, they designed Riviera Country Club, Bel-Air C.C., Los Angeles Country Club (36, originally with Herbert Fowler, redesigned in 1927 by Thomas-Bell), Ojai Valley Inn, Stanford G.C., and La Cumbre C.C. Thomas also financed the completion of his 36-hole municipal course design at Griffith Park. Thomas was an internationally recognized rose hybridizer who also wrote two books on roses and one on deep sea fishing. He was a founding member of Pine Valley.

Stanley Thompson (1894–1952) A member of a noted Canadian golfing family, Thompson is best known for his early work at the breathtaking Banff Springs Hotel course and at Jasper Park Golf Club in Alberta. Thompson was a fine tournament player who believed that the strategic school was the only true form of golf course design. Besides his two courses in Alberta, Thompson's St. George's in Ontario, Canada and Ladies' Golf Club of Toronto stand out as his best works.

A.W. Tillinghast (1874–1942) Tillinghast didn't start designing courses until his early thirties. To that point, he had been a well-established player, receiving his first golf lesson from Old Tom Morris during a stay at St. Andrews in the mid-1890s. In 1916 Tillinghast helped establish the PGA of America, the very first organization dedicated to golf professionals, and to date the only such group of its kind. Tillinghast's first design commission at Shawnee-on-the-Delaware helped him start his own design company. After his Baltusrol Golf Club design opened in 1922, Tillinghast designed the two courses at Winged Foot, and by 1930 his résumé of classic courses was impressive: Ridgewood, Baltusrol, and Somerset Hills in New Jersey; Sleepy Hollow and Quaker Ridge in New York; San Francisco Golf Club in California; and Brook Hollow in Texas; with redesigns of Newport in Rhode Island and Brooklawn in New York. His final significant commission was at Bethpage Park, where he helped create the finest municipal golf complex in the United States. Tillinghast was a prolific writer, though he never actually published a book on golf architecture. He did self-publish two books of his fictional stories, *Cobble Valley Golf Yarns* in 1915 and *The Mutt* in 1925.

Henry Newton Wethered (1869–1955) Sire of British golf prodigies Joyce and Roger Wethered, "H.N." co-authored *The Architectural Side of Golf* with Tom Simpson and another classic, *The Perfect Golfer*. He is the only non-architect quoted in this book.

SOURCES

BOOKS

Hazards, Alec Bauer

Golf Course Architecture, H.S. Colt and C.H. Alison

The Golf Courses of the British Isles, Bernard Darwin

Aspects of Golf Course Architecture, Fred Hawtree

The Links, Robert Hunter

Secrets of the Masters, Bobby Jones (edited by Sidney Matthew)

Golf Is My Game, Bobby Jones

Scotland's Gift—Golf, C.B. Macdonald

Golf Architecture, Alister MacKenzie

The Spirit of St. Andrews, Alister MacKenzie

Wry Stories on the Road Hole, Sid Matthew

The Making of the Masters, David Owen

The Story of Augusta National Golf Club, Clifford Roberts

Golf Has Never Failed Me, Donald Ross

The Book of the Links, Martin Sutton

Golf Architecture in America, George C. Thomas Jr.

The Course Beautiful, A.W. Tillinghast (compiled by Bob Trebus, Stuart Wolffe, and Rick Wolffe)

Reminiscences of the Links, A.W. Tillinghast (compiled by Bob Trebus, Stuart Wolffe, Rick Wolffe)

Gleanings from the Wayside, A.W. Tillinghast (compiled by Bob Trebus, Stuart Wolffe, and Rick Wolffe)

The Architectural Side of Golf, H.N Wethered and Tom Simpson

The Architects of Golf, Ron Whitten and Geoffrey Cornish

PUBLICATIONS

Golf Illustrated (United States)

The American Golfer

Golf Illustrated (United Kingdom)

The Country Club and Pacific Golf and Motor Magazine

The Fairway

Golfing

The United States Golf Association Green Section Bulletin

Country Life

Scribners

ACKNOWLEDGMENTS

The author would like to thank the following for their suggestions, support, guidance, tips, and general wonderfulness: everyone at the Amateur Athletic Foundation, Saundra Sheffer, Jon Winokur, Sid Matthew, Daniel Wexler, Gil Hanse, Patty Moran, and the other sources who helped dig up the material in this book. At Ann Arbor Media Group, sincere thanks to Skip DeWall, Carol Bokas, and Lynne Johnson for continuing to produce great golf books. And a big thank-you to Bill Coore, whose periodic phone calls in search of a great old quote gave me the idea for this book.